Though Justice Sleeps

Sleeps

AFRICAN AMERICANS
1880-1900

THE YOUNG OXFORD HISTORY OF
AFRICAN AMERICANS

Robin D. G. Kelley and Earl Lewis
General Editors

Though Justice Sleeps

AFRICAN AMERICANS
1880-1900

Barbara Bair

Oxford University Press
New York • Oxford

For Judy and her children, Erin and Charley

Oxford University Press

Oxford   New York
Athens Auckland Bangkok Bogotá Bombay
Buenos Aires Calcutta Cape Town Dar es Salaam Delhi
Florence Hong Kong Istanbul Karachi
Kuala Lumpur Madras Madrid Melbourne
Mexico City Nairobi Paris Singapore
Taipei Tokyo Toronto
and associated companies in
Berlin   Ibadan

Published by Oxford University Press, Inc.,
198 Madison Avenue, New York, New York 10016

Library of Congress Cataloging-in-Publication Data
Bair, Barbara
Though justice sleeps : African Americans, 1880 to 1900 / Barbara Bair.
p. cm. — (The young Oxford history of African Americans ; v.6)
Includes bibliographical references and index.
ISBN 0-19-509343-7 (library ed.); ISBN 0-19-508502-7 (series, library ed.)
1. Afro-Americans—History—1877–1964—Juvenile literature.
2. United States—History—1865–1898—Juvenile literature.
[1. Afro-Americans—History—1877–1964.
2. United States—History—1865–1898.]
I. Series.
E185.6.B15   1997
973'.0496073—dc20   96-8472
CIP

3 5 7 9 8 6 4 2

Printed in the United States of America
on acid-free paper

Design: Sandy Kaufman
Layout: Leonard Levitsky
Picture research: Lisa Kirchner, Laura Kreiss

On the cover: Kept In, by Edward Lamson Henry, 1889
Frontispiece: Frederick Douglass Series No. 31, Jacob Lawrence, 1938-39
Page 9: Detail from *The Contribution of the Negro to Democracy in America,* (1943) by Charles White, 11'9" x 17'3"
Hampton University Museum, Hampton, Virginia.

CONTENTS

ROBIN D. G. KELLEY
EARL LEWIS

INTRODUCTION

"The slave went free; stood a brief moment in the sun; then moved back again toward slavery." This is how W. E. B. Du Bois, the great black scholar and activist, described the plight of black people in 1877—the year Reconstruction officially came to a close. Federal troops were withdrawn from the South, freed slaves were not given the land promised them, white terrorist groups ran rampant, and the same defenders of slavery who led the Civil War against the North returned to positions of power. It was a sad moment, for it marked the end of a decade and a half of efforts to create a true democracy in the South. And during the next fifteen years, things only got worse.

It did not have to be this way, Du Bois argued. If only poor whites recognized that their own freedom was tied to the freedom of black people. If they only understood the power of united action, of black and white working together to overthrow the landlords, the merchants, and money-hungry factory owners. Instead, tragically, white people barely able to make ends meet chose allegiance to their race over their class—in other words, they identified more with being white than being a worker or a farmer who shared common interests with black workers and farmers. Thus begins what one historian calls "the nadir" or low point of African-American history.

Low point indeed. Lynchings increased, racial segregation became law, and African-American citizens who worked so hard for the Republican party in the days of Reconstruction found themselves without the right to vote. Many, many emancipated black people found themselves with no property, working for white landlords under conditions reminiscent of slavery. These rural folk had to rent their land, grow the crops the market demanded, and give half or more of what they produced to their landlords. This system of sharecropping, sometimes called the new slavery, kept most African Americans in debt and poverty.

As this volume's title suggests, between 1880 and 1900 it seems as though justice was indeed asleep. But *Though Justice Sleeps* also suggests that African Americans themselves were wide awake, finding ways to fight back and transform the nation that had turned its back on them. Some African Americans joined interracial movements such as the Populists or the Knights of Labor; others turned inward and built religious, fraternal, educational, and political institutions that ultimately became sources of power and inspiration for the stony road ahead. Others simply left, finding refuge as far away as Liberia (West Africa), Canada, and Haiti, or as close as Kansas and Oklahoma. There, African-American men and women founded all-black towns such as Mound Bayou in Mississippi or Langston and Boley in Oklahoma, and imagined a promised land free of white terrorism. A handful followed the advice of black educator Booker T. Washington, who called on Southern black folk to "cast down their buckets where they are" and carve out a life on the land. Proving that African Americans are a productive people, he believed, would reduce the terror and eliminate racism. Then there were those, such as Ida B. Wells, who believed blacks should cast down the gauntlet and punch it out with white supremacists. Wells, one of many leading black women activists of that era, declared war on lynching and sexual violence against black women.

During the later years of the 19th century the creation of several all-black towns in Kansas and Oklahoma encouraged many African Americans to leave the South in search of a land free from the terrors and indignities of white racism.

COME!

To the Colored People of the United States of America:

This is to lay before your minds a few sketches of what great advantages there are for the great mass of people of small means that are emigrating West to come and settle in the county of Hodgeman, in the State of Kansas—and more especially the Colored people, for they are the ones that want to find the best place for climate and for soil for the smallest capital. Hodgeman county is in Southwestern Kansas, on the line of the Atchison, Topeka & Santa Fe Railroad.

We, the undersigned, having examined the above county

Though Justice Sleeps demonstrates that black people were more than victims of Jim Crow laws and racial violence. They organized, fought back, moved around, thought, wrote, and created works of art. They connected their struggles with the rest of the world, turning to Africa, Europe, and the Caribbean for guidance and inspiration. And in many respects, they kept alive a vision of justice and equality born during Reconstruction—a vision that would ultimately shape the entire 20th century.

Though Justice Sleeps is part of an eleven-volume series that narrates African-American history from the 15th through the 20th centuries. Since the 1960s, a rapid explosion in research on black Americans has significantly modified previous understanding of that experience. Studies of slavery, African-American culture, social protest, families, and religion, for example, silenced those who had previously labelled black Americans insignificant historical actors. The new research followed a general upsurge of interest in the social and cultural experiences of the supposedly powerless men and women who did not control the visible reins of power. The result has been a careful and illuminating portrait of how ordinary people make history and serve as the architects of their own destinies.

This series explores many aspects of the lives of African Americans. It describes how black people shaped and changed the history of this nation. It also places the lives of African Americans in the context of the Americas as a whole. We start the story more than a century before the day in 1619 when 19 "negars" stepped off a slave ship in Jamestown, Virginia, and end with the relationship between West Indian immigrants and African Americans in large urban centers like New York in the late 20th century.

At the same time, the series addresses a number of interrelated questions: What was life like for the first Africans to land in the Americas? Were all Africans and African Americans enslaved? How did race shape slavery and how did slavery influence racism? The series also considers questions about male-female relationships, the forging of African-American communities, religious beliefs and practices, the experiences of the young, and the changing nature of social protest. The key events in American history are here, too, but viewed from the perspective of African Americans. The result is a fascinating and compelling story of nearly five centuries of African-American history.

By emphasizing the importance of industrial or vocational education, Booker T. Washington, the founder of the Tuskegee Institute, touched off a fierce debate over the best approach to providing education to black people.

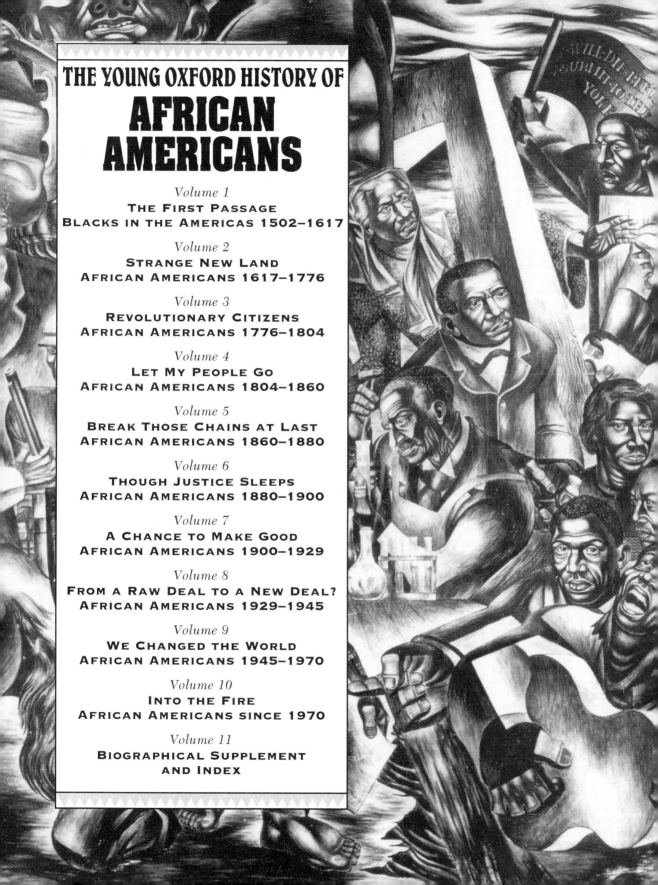

THE YOUNG OXFORD HISTORY OF
AFRICAN AMERICANS

NEGOTIATING FREEDOM

◇ ◇ ◇

When the African-American novelist Frances E. W. Harper wrote the novel *Iola Leroy* in 1892, she created a scene in which the heroine's family discusses their memories of the Civil War and the state of the world in the years that came after it. "I am glad," says Iola's brother Robert, "for the whole nation's sake, that slavery has been destroyed."

"Slavery," Iola Leroy's mother quietly observes, "is dead, but the spirit which animated it still lives." "The problem of the nation," a visiting doctor replies, "is not what men will do with the negro, but what will they do with the reckless, lawless white men who murder, lynch, and burn their fellow-citizens. . . . Our work," he concluded, "is to build over the desolations of the past a better and brighter future. . . . A people cannot habitually trample on law and justice without retrograding toward barbarism."

In creating this fictional discussion, Frances Harper voiced the dilemma of the era. African Americans who had been held in slavery in the United States for generations were officially freed from bondage when Abraham Lincoln's Emancipation Proclamation went into effect in January 1863. But the President's order that slavery be ended was just the beginning of a long process of negotiation about what freedom for African Americans would and should mean.

The period of Reconstruction that followed the end of the Civil War was a time of both tremendous promise and the deep conflict of ideas. At stake was the question of what the racial future of America would be.

Reconstruction began at the close of the war in 1865 and lasted until 1877, when the federal government removed the troops that were still present in the South. Reconstruction was a political process involving a series

A group of children gather for an Emancipation Day celebration in Aiken, South Carolina, in 1888. Though slavery was legally abolished by Abraham Lincoln's Emancipation Proclamation in 1863, true freedom and equality would prove long in coming for most African Americans.

of laws and government decisions by which the South was reintegrated into national politics and restructured to deal with the changes and losses wrought by its defeat in the war.

Those people, black and white, who had fought for the abolition of slavery during the war sought reforms during Reconstruction. They wanted to enact laws and amendments to the U.S. Constitution that would ensure freedom for African Americans by granting them full citizenship rights. They wanted African Americans, the great majority of whom lived in the South, to be able to participate in the political process by voting for candidates and causes they chose. They also wanted them to be able to hold elected office. These political rights were only some of the stepping stones to liberty. African Americans also wanted education for themselves and for their children, and they wanted to be able to farm their own land.

Three key legal actions taken during Reconstruction guaranteed these advances, at least on paper. The 14th Amendment to the Constitution, adopted in July 1868, granted citizenship to all freed people. The 15th Amendment, ratified in May 1870, gave black men the right to cast their

Black members of Congress from the Reconstruction era. During this period, federal laws were passed granting black men the right to vote. With the U.S. Army on hand to enforce the new laws, several Southern states with large black populations elected African Americans to represent them in Congress.

ballots, as only white men before had previously been allowed to do. (African-American women were not included in the provisions of the 15th Amendment, and they, like white women, waited until the 20th century to achieve their right to vote.) In March 1875 the U.S. Congress passed a civil rights act that granted black people equal access to opportunities and rights previously enjoyed only by whites.

Because of these new laws and the presence of the U.S. Army to enforce them, 22 black men were elected from Southern states to serve in the U.S. Congress, and in 1872 an African-American man named Pinckney Pinchback became governor of Louisiana. The Freedmen's Bureau established schools, and African Americans lobbied for what was popularly called "forty acres and a mule"—enough land and means to raise crops to independently support a family.

Unfortunately, the bright hopes of those who favored reforms and rights for African Americans—and who wanted real change in the economic and political character of the country—were not fulfilled. Beginning with the end of Reconstruction in 1878 and continuing into the 20th century, compromises between the federal government and Southern state governments reversed the gains that had been made by blacks in civil and economic rights. Just as bad, sharecropping, the new system that replaced slavery as a means of raising crops in the South, placed millions of African-American families under the thumb of wealthy white landowners. White violence against African Americans also worked to curb black people's personal liberties through threats and fear.

But African Americans did not give up. They continued to negotiate their freedom, step by step. Some rebelled against the sharecropping system by migrating west, where they formed their own towns and homesteads. Others organized groups to travel to Africa with hopes of settling and making a better life in another country. Denied access to jobs, they built their own businesses. Some tried forming unions to protect the jobs they did have. They joined hands and received spiritual strength in their churches. And they spoke out. They founded their own newspapers and used them to express black people's points of view, and they formed organizations—academic societies, women's clubs, business leagues, benevolent associations—that provided for and promoted their own welfare and openly challenged insulting and misleading stereotypes. In all these ways, African Americans were negotiating their freedom and laying a path for future generations to do the same.

All Colored People

THAT WANT TO

GO TO KANSAS,

On September 5th, 1877,

Can do so for $5.00

IMMIGRATION.

WHEREAS, We, the colored people of Lexington, Ky,. knowing that there is an abundance of choice lands now belonging to the Government, have assembled ourselves together for the purpose of locating on said lands. Therefore,

BE IT RESOLVED, That we do now organize ourselves into a Colony, as follows:— Any person wishing to become a member of this Colony can do so by paying the sum of one dollar ($1.00), and this money is to be paid by the first of September, 1877, in instalments of twenty-five cents at a time, or otherwise as may be desired.

RESOLVED, That this Colony has agreed to consolidate itself with the Nicodemus Towns, Solomon Valley, Graham County, Kansas, and can only do so by entering the vacant lands now in their midst, which costs $5.00.

RESOLVED, That this Colony shall consist of seven officers—President, Vice-President, Secretary, Treasurer, and three Trustees. President—M. M. Bell; Vice-President —Isaac Talbott; Secretary—W. J. Niles; Treasurer—Daniel Clarke; Trustees—Jerry Lee, William Jones, and Abner Webster.

RESOLVED, That this Colony shall have from one to two hundred militia, more or less, as the case may require, to keep peace and order, and any member failing to pay in his dues, as aforesaid, or failing to comply with the above rules in any particular, will not be recognized or protected by the Colony.

CHAPTER 1

LAND: "I WILL HAVE A HOME"
◇ ◇ ◇

You can talk about the latest, the latest of your homes . . .
One time I seen a Boll Weevil, he was settin' on a square,
Next time I seen the Boll Weevil, he had his whole family there,
He was lookin' for a home, he was lookin' for a home.

The farmer take the Boll Weevil, put him in the sand,
The Boll Weevil said to the farmer, "You treat me just like a man.
And I'll have a home, and I'll have a home."

Now the [tenant] farmer he said to the merchant, "I never made but one bale,
Before I'll let you have that last one, I will suffer and die in jail,
I will have a home, I will have a home.

—Leadbelly, "The Tale of Boll Weevil"

The vast amounts of land available in Western territories such as Kansas and Oklahoma offered many Southern blacks the hope of someday living and working on their own land. This notice was posted in Lexington, Kentucky.

J ohn Solomon Lewis and his wife had worked the same land in Louisiana for years. Each year they brought in large crops, but at the end of the harvest, when they made the payments they owed, they would find themselves further in debt. They sought release from this burden of labor without reward by moving to a new home in Kansas. When they arrived in the new place they experienced a feeling of jubilation that they had not felt since the end of slavery some 15 years before. The earth and sky seemed free to them in Kansas— free and beautiful, and open to possibilities that they had ceased to hope for in Louisiana. Much as slaves who fled their bondage before emancipation had rejoiced in successfully escaping from the South, the Lewises thanked God for their deliverance. "When I knew I had all my family in a free land," John Solomon Lewis said, "I said let us hold a little prayer meeting; so we held a little meeting on the river bank. It was raining but the drops fell from heaven on a free family, and the meeting was just as

15

good as sunshine. We was thankful to God for ourselves and we prayed for those who could not come."

The Lewises and other like them began from a desperate condition. In the last two decades of the 19th century, 9 out of 10 of the 6.5 million African Americans in the United States made their homes in the South. Eighty percent of these black Southerners lived in rural areas, and most of them were farmers or agricultural laborers. Some were landowners and had their own small farms, but most were tenants. They rented the land where they worked for cash or a share of the crops they raised. Others worked for hire.

Around the beginning of each year, a tenant farming family would enter into a contract to rent a small portion of a former plantation or a farm, usually about 15 to 20 acres, to cultivate a crop, most often cotton. The amount of acreage varied according to the size of the family. Money rarely changed hands between the landlord and the family. Instead, the rent for the land would be paid to the landowner in bales of cotton. The worth of the cotton and the amount that each family could grow depended on such things as the price of cotton on the market and the quality of the soil in which the tenant family tried to produce a crop. This kind of farming arrangement, in which rent to landowners was paid with a share of the crop, was called sharecropping. After paying for implements and animals— farm tools, a plow, mules to pull the plow—and rent for the land, the tenants were typically left with their share of the arrangement, about one-third of the profit from the sale of the cotton they had grown.

In 1878 the Puckett family of Tensas Parish, Louisiana, rented 25 acres of land. The Pucketts and their children worked 22 of these acres in the cash crop, cotton, and another 3 in corn. Rent was figured at 10 bales of cotton: 5 bales were paid or "shared" for the rent of the land, 2 bales for the use of two mules, 2 for the feed the mules ate during the year, and 1 bale for borrowing the tools necessary to grow and harvest the crop. From the sale of the cotton that was produced in addition to these 10 bales, the Pucketts needed to reserve enough money to purchase seed cotton for the next year's crop. Most tenants also owed money to a storekeeper for wares purchased on credit during the months before the cotton was picked and delivered to the local market. The prices that storekeepers set on basic staples like molasses, cornmeal, and flour were high, and tenant farmers also paid interest (extra charges) on what they purchased on credit (the store owners kept a record of all the items a family had purchased during the

A black family at work picking cotton in the 1880s. The biased terms many blacks were subjected to as sharecroppers made it very difficult for them to make a profit from their work.

year and charged them for it when the harvest came in and cotton was ginned, baled, and sold). Some of the tenant farmers mortgaged, or borrowed money in exchange for, their crops to pay their landlords or the storekeepers what they owed from the past. That arrangement allowed them to stay on their rented land or to be able to get needed supplies to support their families while they grew the current crop of cotton.

It was very difficult for tenant farmers working under sharecropping arrangements to get ahead financially, and having enough to eat and adequate clothing were always worries. Most faced each new year owing money from years before to the white people from whom they rented land and to the merchant who ran the store where they purchased their goods. "We make as much cotton and sugar as we did when we were slaves," one black tenant farmer in Texas observed, "and it does us as little good now as it did then." Laborers who questioned the high prices charged to them, which would invariably be set at a rate that would encompass or exceed the value of their entire year's crop, had little legal recourse. As one black

Mississippian testified to the Senate, "Colored men soon learn that it is better to pay any account, however unjust, than to refuse, for he stands no possible chance of getting justice before the law."

Many African-American sharecroppers and farmers sought greater justice by moving to different land. When their contracts were up at one place, they would often pack their belongings and enter into a new arrangement on another tract of acreage, hoping to improve over their last year's experience. One Alabama sharecropper reported the frustration she felt when she went out in the moonlight to plant rosebushes to beautify the plot of land she was renting, never knowing whose yard it would be the next year. Some moved even further than from one plot in the neighborhood to another. They migrated from the South to form new, black towns in the West, or dreamed of a life of justice and independence in an all-black Africa.

Leaving, for families already in debt and under white economic control, was no easy matter. It was hard to do without much money, and it could be dangerous. White Southerners did not want black laborers to leave, because their low-paid work made white economic gains possible. During the great exodus of African Americans to Kansas in 1879–81,

Settlers of Nicodemus, Kansas, stand in front of their general store in 1885. Nicodemus was just one of many all-black towns that were formed in Kansas during this period.

North-bound steamboats operated by whites would refuse to pick up black migrants waiting for passage to St. Louis, and groups of black travelers were stranded for weeks along the river without shelter. They found it difficult to locate white merchants who would sell them food. Some were jailed, accused of owing money to whites. If they had been carrying cash to pay for passage and relocation for their families when they were arrested, it could be taken from them by white marshals before they entered their cells and not returned upon their release. Others were accosted by groups of whites who stole their wagons or horses from them, or did them bodily harm. A U.S. Army officer named Thomas Conway, who reviewed conditions along the Mississippi River, reported to President Rutherford B. Hayes that "every river landing is blockaded by white enemies of the colored exodus; some of whom are mounted and armed, as if we are at war."

Indeed, some of the migrants went not so much for the lure of land but to escape violence. Several African Americans whose testimony was part of a U.S. Senate investigation of the migrations in 1880 cited personal knowledge of violent acts committed by whites against blacks as their main reason for leaving. A farmer named George Rogers, who had taken his family from Louisiana to Kansas, told of a young neighbor who was riddled with bullets by a group of white men who broke into his home in Madison Parish, Louisiana. He was shot before his mother's eyes because "he was a smart boy and read the papers, and the white people there won't allow that." White people who committed these acts of terrorism or forced black residents off their land were known as "regulators" or "bulldozers."

Sixty-three-year-old Edward Parlor and his wife left Warren County, Mississippi, after a neighbor woman who had planned to move to Kansas was attacked by white men. Pregnant at the time of the attack, she was raped and then hanged by a rope and left to die. Women were sometimes more forthright than men in stating that the reason for their wanting to go elsewhere was because of their fear that they or their daughters would be the targets of white sexual assault.

Those who did leave and were marooned in St. Louis without enough funds to go further took refuge with black families, and relief to send the stranded on their way was organized through mass meetings in black churches and relief boards set up by black ministers and community leaders. Despite the risks involved, thousands of laborers and middle-class people desirous of greater opportunities left for Kansas, Oklahoma, and other areas outside the South. "The word it has been spoken; the message has been sent," wrote abolitionist and women's rights activist Sojourner Truth in verse she composed about the migrations: "The prison doors have opened, and out the prisoners went." For Truth and other older activists who had worked hard to bring about the end of slavery, the post-Reconstruction treks to new lands were seen as one more step in the march toward real emancipation. For other leaders, such as Frederick Douglass, the migrations were a mistake. Douglass felt that African Americans should remain where they were, confront violence, and take a stand for equal rights. This was difficult to do, and while many African Americans did work and speak out to change conditions in the regions where they lived, others, particularly the poor, who lived under harsh circumstances, longed to escape rather than place their hopes in reforming political and economic systems that were so weighed against them.

Frederick Douglass, the celebrated abolitionist, author, and lecturer, believed strongly that blacks should fight for equal rights where they were, and not separate themselves from whites. Douglass devoted his life to the fight against slavery and to the cause of equal rights for blacks.

Some black leaders argued that the federal government should make public lands available to black settlement as compensation for the centuries that Americans of African descent had spent in slavery. In 1887 William H. Thomas wrote in the African Methodist Episcopal *Church Review* that he saw the involvement of the government in the distribution of land as an issue of morality and legal principle, mandated by the "equity of justice between man and man, and government and citizen." If slavery was wrong, Thomas argued, then "Negroes were illegally held to service; some measure of compensation, therefore, is due them, not only from individuals who were the nominal owners, but from the National Government which was the prime factor in their enslavement and maintenance in bondage. . . . No measure of compensation would work such beneficial results to the free people," Thomas concluded, "as the ownership of land." Thomas, like many others who had come before and would follow him, proposed the creation of a separate black territory or state within the United States. In Thomas's vision, the government would buy expanses of land in Southern states and divide their acreage into small homesteads that would be made available for black settlement.

At the same time that Thomas was making his proposals, Edward (also called Edwin) P. McCabe, a black politician from Kansas, hoped to establish a black territory in the West. He encouraged black migration to lands in Oklahoma Territory that had been newly opened to settlement by non-Indians in the late 1880s. He hoped enough black people would respond to the land rush there that voting majorities of blacks would be created in the territory's local districts. African Americans who came would own land and businesses, and would be able to govern themselves.

The longing for land and political control that beckoned laborers and middle-class investors west also made them think of Africa. In the last decade of the century, while the populations of black towns like Mound Bayou, Mississippi, and Edward P. McCabe's Langston City in Oklahoma Territory continued to grow, contingents of black families from Oklahoma and Arkansas made their way from Western homes to New York City in hopes of securing passage to Liberia, on the west coast of Africa.

Henry Adams and Benjamin Singleton were among the African-American activists who advocated mass black emigration from the South in the late 1870s and 1880s. These advocates contacted organizations founded to provide passage to African Americans who wanted to move to West Africa, including the long-established (and white-dominated) American Colonization Society and several newer enterprises such as the black-administered Liberian Exodus Joint Stock Steamship Company. Gathering support from tens of thousands of rural black Southerners, Adams and other organizers like him viewed Liberia as a potential home for working people with agricultural skills.

A church and other buildings built by American missionaries in Liberia. African Americans first began settling in Liberia in 1822. During the years after Reconstruction, more and more African Americans viewed Liberia as a place where educated blacks might thrive.

Other African Americans, especially middle-class leaders, saw West Africa not so much as a place to escape from
white violence or as a land of opportunity for workers with
few resources, but as a place where educated blacks of
African and African-American origin could develop their own
business enterprises and political structures. In the mid-1880s
and 1890s, grassroots groups like Benjamin Singleton's United
Transatlantic Society, based in Tennessee and Kansas, continued to advocate migration to Africa as a means of racial unity
and progress at the same time that they encouraged Southern
blacks to move westward. In a June 1885 circular, Singleton
declared that moving would help "establish the true social
equality which justice demands wherever the foot of an
African treads the soil."

For ordinary blacks caught in the grips of the tenant
land and credit systems and living in fear of white lawlessness and harm, the hope of gaining justice of any kind—
either political or economic—within the United States
seemed elusive. Some used metaphors of family to describe their interest in traveling to their motherland, Africa.
"We feel like children away from home," one man named
Jackson, who lived in Georgia, wrote to an official of the
American Colonization Society in June 1891: "We are quite
sure that the U.S. of America is not the place for the colored
man." Another man wrote from Mississippi to a colonization
society in the East, comparing the repression he and the
black people he knew were experiencing to the conditions
faced in times of bondage: We are not "anything but slaves"
here, he said, "and cant get out . . . Oh my God help us
to get out from here to Africa."

Bishop Henry McNeal Turner, a leader of the African Methodist
Episcopal Church and an advocate of black emigration, was a public
spokesman for the longings of this man and others like him. He had traveled to Liberia and wrote and spoke of its promise. Organizers for the
American Colonization Society also toured through the South, speaking at
churches and community centers about African heritage and black nation-
hood in Africa. When African Americans read Turner's letters about
Liberia that were published in church newspapers in 1891, they responded.

Benjamin Singleton was one of the leaders of the movement advocating black emigration from the South. Singleton led thousands of blacks to all-black communities he established in Kansas, Okla-homa, and Colorado.

Black Cherokee residents of Muldrow and Redland in Indian Territory organized a migration club and distributed leaflets published by the colonization society. With great enthusiasm they held frequent meetings over the next year. They sold their farms and possessions and left by railroad for New York, prepared to sail from there to Liberia in March 1892.

Meanwhile, another contingent of African Americans also arrived in New York. They came from Arkansas, a state where many people had heard of Turner's dream of a new life for American blacks in Liberia. Like the citizens of Muldrow and Redland, they had formed local clubs to encourage emigration. Many people wrote to inquire about securing passage or came East in hope of boarding a transatlantic steamer, but the colonization society did not have enough boats to carry them or the funding to promise future voyages. These disappointed travelers became temporary urban refugees. They either returned West or made homes in the city.

While the influence of the colonization society declined as a result of its financial hardships and administrative reorganization after 1892, several

These refugees from Arkansas made their way to New York City in 1880 hoping to find transportation to Liberia. They were housed temporarily at the Mount Olivet Baptist Chapel.

independent movements were formed in the 1890s. Emigration remained an important topic of discussion among lower- and working-class African Americans.

Small groups of immigrants successfully left for Africa, but the overwhelming majority of African Americans remained in the United States. Many who wanted to go to Africa could not afford to pay for the passage. If they decided to leave the South, they looked instead for places relatively close to home to secure land and contribute their labor. Since the late 1870s, black people from Kentucky, Missouri, and Tennessee had been establishing new lives in Kansas and in small settlements on the Western prairies. Just as national proponents of African repatriation visited churches and schools to teach African Americans about Africa and the possibility of going there, so promoters of migration clubs who wanted to encourage relocation to the West organized through existing black social institutions.

A circular issued by Benjamin Singleton and other officers of the Edgefield Association in Tennessee urged those interested in homesteading—or laying a claim to land by occupying and developing it, rather than buying it for cash—to come out to meetings at the local hall or the Nashville Second Baptist Church to "See What Colored Citizens Are Doing for Their Elevation." The motivation for going to other states was similar to the idea of going to Africa. "We as a people are oppressed and disfranchised," one westward migrant wrote in a letter in 1891. "We are still working hard and our rights taken from us[. T]imes are hard and getting harder every year. We as a people believe that Affrica is the place but to get from under bondage are thinking of Oklahoma as this is our nearest place of safety."

In 1889–90 portions of what was called the Unassigned Lands in Indian Territory and all of Oklahoma Territory (areas that in 1907 would become parts of the state of Oklahoma) were opened to settlement by non-Indian peoples. Indian Territory had been the home of relocated Indian peoples since federal policy had forcibly moved Native Americans from their traditional homelands in the East in the 1830s. Many blacks living in the region were former slaves, or the descendants of those who had been held in bondage by Cherokee, Creek, or other Indian peoples for generations. Many of these freedmen and their families were themselves citizens of the Indian nations. In the early 1890s, African Americans from neighboring Arkansas and other Southern states were attracted to the land grants available in the areas newly opened to settlement by outsiders. More

White, black, and Seminole children attended this integrated school in the Oklahoma Territory. After the area was opened to settlement by non-Indians in 1889–90, blacks and whites rushed to occupy the land.

than 7,000 of them moved. They did so with the hope not only for property, but for political independence.

Several all-black towns were established in the territories. These were places where African Americans could form their own municipal governments and protect one another from white incursions and violence. Langston City was one such town. It had its own newspaper, and when black residents across the South read about the plans for the town, they joined dozens of Oklahoma booster clubs that advertised opportunities and promoted migration. A few hundred came to Langston. In 1897 Langston University (also called the Agricultural and Normal University), a college where black teachers were trained, was established in Langston by the territorial legislature. The town's primary promoter, Edward P. McCabe—the same McCabe who dreamed of establishing a territory of the United States where blacks were in political control—encouraged emigrants to become involved in Republican party politics and to start businesses. McCabe had earlier helped settle the black town of Nicodemus, Kansas, which was

This is to Certify, That

of   County, State of

has this day paid the sum of FIVE DOLLARS, being the full amount of Membership Fees in the

Nicodemus Town Company of Graham Co., Kansas,

and that said   is entitled to any vacant Town Lot on the town site of Nicodemus, Graham County, Kansas, at the time said party arrives at Nicodemus; the said Nicodemus Town Company giving their obligation to make Title to said Lot as required by law. And it is further agreed that no Intoxicating Liquors shall be sold on said lot within five years from this date.

Dated at   this   day of   187 .

Not valid until countersigned by W. R. HILL, Gen'l Manager. *Nicodemus Town Company.*
This Certificate should be presented to W. H. SMITH, President.

For a fee of five dollars, black settlers of Nicodemus, Kansas, were granted this certificate entitling them to any vacant lot in the town. The chance to own their own land was a powerful lure for many African Americans.

named for an African prince who was brought to the American colonies as a slave and later purchased his own freedom.

Most newly arrived residents in the West and Midwest lived in simple dugouts and took up subsistence farming, much like the African Americans who were already living in the region. A more prosperous middle class also emerged, and these people operated hotels, blacksmith shops, barbershops, saloons, and other service-oriented establishments. Other blacks became deputy marshals or worked on ranches as cowboys and wranglers. Black churches, women's groups, and fraternal orders were founded. By 1900, more than 55,000 African Americans were living in Oklahoma and Indian territories, and between 1890 and 1910, 25 black communities were founded in the Oklahoma region. A song written by a man known to local residents as Uncle Jesse celebrated the black economic independence represented by the all-black town of Boley, Oklahoma, which was founded just after the turn of the century:

> Say, have you heard the story,
> Of a little colored town,
> Way over in the [Cherokee] Nation
> On such a lovely sloping ground?
> With as pretty little houses

As you ever chanced to meet,
With not a thing but colored folks
A-standing in the streets?
Oh, 'tis a pretty country
And the Negroes own it, too
With not a single white man here
To tell us what to do—in Boley

Efforts at westward migration and the formation of black towns, like transatlantic emigration to West Africa, were plagued by the relative poverty of the majority of black workers and subsistence farmers. Neither the emigration clubs nor African colonization organizations and companies had funds for long-term investment. Middle-class organizers and developers involved in the black-towns movement and in Liberian colonization schemes tried hard to attract settlers who had the financial capital to start or support businesses, purchase land, and establish long-lasting schools, churches, and civic and social associations. Accomplishing these things was difficult to do for those with little money. Colonists in Africa faced prolonged rainy seasons and types of illnesses and fevers they were not used to, and they often arrived in Africa to find that provisions and resources that had been promised to them were scarce.

Blacks who participated in the westward exoduses purchased more than 20,000 acres of land in Kansas in the early 1880s, but at the same time thousands of individuals arrived after difficult journeys, impoverished, undernourished, and in need of help. For them, basics like seed, clothing, and farming implements were hard to buy. Many took jobs on the railroads or in towns instead of establishing their own small farms as they had hoped to do. Crop failures and droughts made conditions worse. The economic depression of 1893–94 drove down cotton prices and raised interest rates, burying tenant farmers in deeper debt within the credit system, and made cash and jobs even more scarce than before.

Still, there were successes. The presence of a nearby railroad line could make a big difference in a black town's ability to last over time. Mound Bayou, Mississippi, had a railroad depot. Mound Bayou was a town with a majority black population that, like sites further to the west, was founded on the principles of racial pride and economic opportunity. Black citi-

Edward P. McCabe was the primary promoter behind the success of Langston City, Oklahoma, and other cities in the West, but he never realized his dream of establishing a territory of the U.S. where blacks were in political control

zens there were able to steadily increase the number of acres of land under tillage in surrounding farms. They established several commercial business-es, such as cotton gins and sawmills, whose success was linked to the avail-ability of rail transportation that quickly moved products created or processed by the businesses to the market. In the 1890s, the residents of Mound Bayou replaced dugouts and log cabins with wood houses and built five new churches and a school building. Black people were elected as city aldermen and held office as mayor.

In the 1890s the Langston City, Oklahoma, *Herald* newspaper emphasized the desire of town leaders and promoters to attract middle-class people to their town. Ads called for shoemakers and other artisans, and invited those who could begin new businesses such as a lumberyard and a harness shop. Several grocery stores already existed, as did saloons, blacksmiths, barbershops, feed stores, mills, yeast and soap factories, a bank, hotels, and an opera house. The newspaper's editors also promised black readers that political liberty and justice would be by-products of life in Langston. If they came, the "enjoyment of every right and privilege that any other man enjoys under the constitution and laws of our country" would be theirs.

Black settlers in Oklahoma stand in front of the simple dugout shack they called home.

But in the same period when this promise was being made, African Americans saw their political rights increasingly under attack. By the 1890s,

Jim Crow laws segregated people of different races in public places such as schools, restaurants, and theaters. They also applied different rules that affected blacks' and whites' ability to do things like vote, secure loans, or chose a place to live. The term "Jim Crow" was an old pejorative way of referring to black people. It had been in popular use since the 1830s. The Jim Crow laws made areas of the West and Midwest, which at first had seemed attractive, difficult places for blacks to fulfill their dreams of independent lives free of white control or repression.

Despite injustices, people made good lives for themselves and their neighbors. They worked hard, raised families, and looked after one another in their communities. Agnes Rogers Walker (who was known as "Babe") and her husband Dan Walker were among those who had grown up in the Cherokee Nation before other blacks migrated west to settle in nearby towns. In the last decades of the 1800s they farmed land that came to them when the federal government broke up into separate parcels land that had previously been held in common by all the members of the Cherokee Nation and allotted them to individual citizens of the Cherokee Nation. In 1939, when she was an old woman and living in Bartlesville, Oklahoma, Agnes Rogers was interviewed for the Works Progress Administration's Indian-Pioneer History Project. "My parents were former slaves" who before emancipation had had different masters and lived on different farms, she told the woman who interviewed her. "My maternal grandmother was a full blood Cherokee" (a person of Indian heritage whose family members had not intermarried with whites), "and my grandfather was a Negro," she explained. She was born during the Civil War and her family lived in a "one room log cabin with a log summer kitchen" on Rabb's Creek, which was named for her uncle. After the war her parents "settled on my grandmother's allotment of eighty acres" in the Cooweescoowee District of the Cherokee Nation (now Rogers County, Oklahoma), near the town of Talala, Indian Territory. "Our furniture was all home-made with the exception of one bed, and we cooked on a fireplace. My parents [Houston Rogers and Sidney Ross-Rogers] were farmers and we raised most of our living. The chief crops in our vicinity were corn, potatoes, and vegetables. Our principal foods were corn bread, milk, butter, sorghum, hog meat and beef." Her father made his own farming implements. He owned one horse, one yoke (two) of steers, and a plough, harness, and harrow.

The Rogers family's log house was not far from where the Chisholm Trail crossed through Indian Territory, and as a young woman in the 1880s

Agnes Rogers worked as a cook at the white-owned Talala Hotel during the busy seasons when area cattle were brought to local stockyards. She helped farm her family's land and also cooked and did laundry for the large groups of cowhands who worked at a nearby ranch owned by mixed-blood Cherokee elites (an upper-class family of Cherokees who had intermarried with whites). Her father's and uncle's agricultural labor had helped establish the expansive ranch in the years after the Civil War.

Agnes Rogers Walker was one of the African-American women who helped provide health care to other women in the area, including those giving birth. Her husband, Dan Walker, was an expert rider and roper and an essential presence on the large ranch where Agnes also worked. He later became a U.S. deputy marshal. He was from Fort Gibson, Indian Territory, and had come of age in an era when more than 5,000 African Americans, almost all of them men, worked in the West herding cattle, and many others (known to Indians as "Buffalo soldiers" because of the similarity the Indians saw between the men's tightly curled hair and that of the buffalo) served in U.S. Army infantry and calvary regiments stationed in Western states. Dan Walker supervised the treatment of the horses and helped coordinate the herding and branding of the cattle at the ranch where he worked. In the 1880s he taught his children, Charlotte, Charlie, and Mack,

Black cowboys in Texas around 1890. During the last part of the 19th century black cowboys played a large role in the development of the Western economy, participating in cattle drives and working on ranches.

to rope and ride horses. The Walker children "practiced roping and soon Charlotte could rope and ride as well as the boys," Agnes recalled.

With the coming of the railroads and the fencing of the land, the massive trail drives in which African-American cowboys had traditionally found employment gave way to the shipment of cattle by train. In the last part of the 19th century, the proportion of cowboys who were black varied from 25 to 60 percent in different areas of the West. Many of them worked in Texas and Indian Territory. By the late 1880s and early 1890s, these hands—Dan Walker, for example—worked for hire on individual ranches, sometimes farming their own homesteads on the side and raising small herds. Other highly skilled cowboys like Walker entered the roping contest circuit, turning the work they did on the range into performance art. They competed for prize money as horseback riders and ropers in small town exhibitions, large regional expositions, and state and county fairs. Their presence on the roping circuits set the stage for the later achievements of men like Bill Pickett, a black cowboy at the Miller 101 Ranch who became famous for his performances in rodeo and Wild West shows.

Bill Pickett became famous for his performances in rodeo and Wild West shows. Many black cowboys competed for money in contests held throughout the West.

Unlike men who made their living in the cattle industry and its offshoots, women in the West were employed primarily in farming family plots. And, like Agnes Rogers Walker, many were employed in the service economy, working as cooks, cleaners, and laundresses in households and boardinghouses or hotels, raising other people's children, or for a few, working in black-owned stores.

Almost all the married women who migrated to Kansas worked for hire, most often as washerwomen. Steady work was sometimes hard to find, and families moved frequently after their initial exodus, going where they could find jobs. In 1886, a report issued by the Kansas Bureau of Labor and Industrial Statistics stated that the combined average yearly income of black husbands and wives was $363.28, or about the same as a single white male laborer. Yet about three-quarters of black working families owned their own homes. Many educated black women taught school, and women provided community services through their churches and women's neighborhood unions and clubs.

Some women also participated in the "wild" west in a way similar to single men. Mary Fields, a woman who became well known in Montana, was a kind of female equivalent of the adventurous black cowboy, Nat Love (who was also known as Deadwood Dick).

The Shores family of Custer County, Nebraska, in the late 1880s. Women in the rural West helped work their family farms and often contributed to the family income by taking in laundry or working for hire as cooks at nearby ranches.

Fields hauled heavy freight for nuns at a Catholic mission in Cascade, Montana, and later ran a restaurant, but she was best known for her gunplay. She occasionally challenged men to duels and held her own in her conflicts with them. She earned a reputation for her toughness in delivering the United States mail over difficult terrains and in all kinds of weather. Like many black women, she also ran a laundry, but unlike others, she spent her free time smoking and drinking in the local saloon. Although she was unusual in choosing a style of life more typical for men, her life is a good example of the many different kinds of labor Western black women were engaged in, and their involvement in the service economy.

For most black women who remained in the South, the kinds of domestic chores and farm work that they did had not changed much since emancipation. They worked long hours scrubbing floors, cooking and preparing food, sewing, washing, mending, and doing dishes. They cared for their children, and they planted, chopped, and picked cotton and helped with wheat, corn, and tobacco crops. They also grew small gardens or sometimes kept a cow in order to add greens, butter, and milk to the regular family diet of cornmeal, salt pork, and molasses. They often would try to do what they could to earn a little cash: raise chickens and sell the eggs, pick wild berries for market, or take in extra laundry. William Pickens, who became an important educator and officer in the National

Association for the Advancement of Colored People, a civil rights organization founded in 1910, remembered that during his childhood in the 1880s "Mother cooked and washed and Father felled trees in the icy 'brakes' to make rails and boards" to sell to others. While men would usually have the ultimate responsibility for planting and maintaining the crops, and were the ones most likely to negotiate contracts and money matters with white landowners, women's work was multifaceted.

Most African-American households were, like the Walkers', the Pucketts', or the Lewises', headed by a husband and a wife, and on average they had four or five members living under one roof. Men usually were married by the time they were 25 years old, and women by age 20. Hard manual labor, poverty, and poor nutrition among the majority of African Americans who worked as sharecroppers were reflected in low fertility rates (a declining number of babies born per family), high child mortality rates (infants and small children frequently died before they grew up to be adults), and an average life expectancy for black men and women of just 33 years. Many families lived near other kin, and as women and men grew older they often took into their households other relatives and boarders from outside their immediate family. In addition to caring for her family, a woman living in the rural South would also be involved in working with other women in her neighborhood, just as Agnes Rogers Walker did in Indian Territory. She would help out in times of illness or childbirth, or lend a hand when extra labor was required or someone needed to be looked after.

Some African-American families left agricultural life behind completely. Moving to the city, like migration west and repatriation to Africa, was one of the forms of movement that African Americans engaged in as they searched for a better life. While tenant farmers or sharecroppers would often move from one plot of rented land to another, country people also moved from farms to small towns and from towns to cities. In the 1880s and 1890s, although four-fifths of African Americans still lived in rural areas, the concentration of black populations in the urban parts of the South and of black workers in industries continually increased. For them, it was not land but work that was the focus of their search for equality and rights.

CHAPTER 2

LABOR: "LET US PUT OUR SHOULDERS TO THE WHEEL"

◇ ◇ ◇

I am a colored man. . . . I would say to my people, Help the cause of labor. I would furthermore say to colored men, Organize. . . . You are a man. Let us break this race prejudice which capital likes. Let us put our shoulders to the wheel, men, and victory is ours.

—Anonymous member of the Knights of Labor, writing to John Swinton's Paper, October 10, 1886

I n a letter published in the *United Mine Workers Journal* on July 14, 1892, African-American union organizer Richard L. Davis talked about the rights of working people and addressed some thoughts to those who saw solutions for blacks in migration or back-to-Africa movements. "The negro has a right in this country," Davis wrote, "They are here and to stay."

One of the places that African Americans were staying was in the cities of the South. Some black urban residents had been in the cities since before the Civil War, when they worked either as slaves or as free men and women. Others came or were born there in the last decades of the 1800s, when the numbers of black people in large Southern urban centers grew. In 1880, for example, the U.S. census showed 16,337 black people living in Nashville, Tennessee. They made up 38 percent of the total population of the city. By the time of the next U.S. census, in 1890, there were 29,395 blacks in Nashville, comprising 39 percent of the city's population. While African-American citizens were still a minority in Nashville in 1890, they made up more than half the populations of other cities, including Montgomery, Alabama, and Raleigh, North Carolina.

Although in this period only a small percentage of the black population of the United States lived in Northern states, of those who did, most

Merchants and shoppers at the old Center Market in Washington, D.C., in 1889. African Americans joined other urban dwellers in buying, selling, and exchanging goods, including eggs and produce from vegetable gardens, near the heart of the capital's downtown.

lived in cities. In the great migration movements of the 1900s, many black people moved to major industrial urban centers like Chicago, Detroit, and New York, but in the 1880s and 1890s, Philadelphia had the largest number of black residents of any of the Northern cities. In 1880, 32,000 African Americans were living in Philadelphia, and by 1900, 63,000 black people made their homes there and accounted for 4 percent of the city's population as a whole. Proportionately small but significant black populations also lived in the Southern-Northern border city of Washington, D.C., in Baltimore, Maryland, the New England city of Boston, and other urban areas of the North.

For African Americans in the cities, North and South, as for share-croppers in the country, employment helped determine the way marriages and families were organized. Severe racial discrimination affected where African Americans could live within cities. Racism also limited black people to a small number of occupations, mostly very poorly paid. These conditions made options regarding marriage and family for black people different than those of their white counterparts.

Life was very difficult for the white urban poor also, especially for recent immigrants from Europe who were impoverished and subjected to ethnic prejudice from native-born whites. But while employment options expanded for American-born whites and white-ethnic immigrants, especially in factory and industrial work, opportunities for African Americans in the cities became even more narrowly defined in the 1880s and 1890s.

Earlier in the century, most free black men and male slaves (and, after the Civil War, ex-slaves) who worked in the cities were manual laborers. A significant proportion of men also worked in skilled positions or as artisans and in construction trades such as carpentry and masonry. Richard R. Wright, who became a social scientist, recalled that when he was a young man in Savannah, Georgia, he could walk down the streets and see black carpenters, bricklayers, and wood sawyers at work. Much of the construction of the public works and transportation systems that made Southern cities function, their "railroads and streets . . . sewers and water works," Wright remembered, were "largely constructed by Negroes." Over time, however, black men were increasingly excluded from the trades and the variety of their presence in the city work world was diminished.

The racism that grew more overt in the last two decades of the 1800s meant greater segregation, restriction, and exclusion of black men from apprentice opportunities and from higher-paid skilled types of work. Some

A crew of blacks, supervised by a white man, working on railroad tracks near Spencer, North Carolina, around 1890.

black men in the cities continued to work as artisans—as shoemakers, blacksmiths, coopers (barrel makers), bakers, and barbers. Indeed, one of the most famous shoemakers of the era was an African-American named Jan Matzeliger who lived in Lynn, Massachusetts. He revolutionized the shoemaking trade when he invented a machine that he patented in 1883. His lasting machine shaped and stitched the upper portion of a shoe to its sole, something that previously had to be done by hand.

Despite their skill and achievement, black artisans and small shop-keepers were increasingly segregated and saw white patronage disappear. They found their customers among the growing number of African Americans coming to the cities, many of whom were very poor. Although there were very successful black businessmen and -women who achieved wealth, it was difficult for most black artisans and shopkeepers to make enough money to achieve middle-class status. Most of the relatively small number of middle-class blacks who made up the elite of African-Americans in the cities were professionals—teachers, doctors, or lawyers—or were employed in white-collar government work.

The majority of black men in the urban work force after 1880—about 75 percent—were confined to manual labor positions or jobs in personal service. The laborers were stevedores (who unloaded the cargo of ships), sailors, hod carriers (who carried supplies like mortar or brick to bricklayers, stonemasons, and others at a construction work site), janitors, and the people who did the heavy labor rebuilding city streets or installing public works such as sewer lines. One-third of the African Americans in Philadelphia in the late 1890s worked as servants. They were house servants, valets, and coachmen, porters (who carried purchases for shoppers in large stores or provided assistance to travelers on trains), hotel help, or waiters. Men made more money in personal service occupations than manual laborers or women in similar service jobs. Given the more strenuous alternatives for employment, they formed a kind of social elite who tended to look down upon those who made a living in ways that involved more dirt and brawn.

Women, too, were restricted in the types of jobs they were allowed to do. The majority of African-American women worked in household service or as laundresses or washerwomen. A few were dressmakers, hatmakers, seamstresses, typists, nurses, or teachers, but it was difficult to get these kinds of work because of white prejudice. White shopgirls or office workers would refuse to work beside black women, and white women would not patronize black women who had skills to offer in health care or fashion. Prostitution was also an urban occupation for women. Like live-in personal service, it was a way of making a living that made childraising difficult.

African-American women had few choices of jobs available to them. Many black women worked in white households as maids or nannies, as did this woman from Washington, D.C.

One out of five African-American residents of cities, men and women combined, worked as domestic servants within white households. Though many went home at night from these jobs, significant numbers lived in the household where they worked, separated from their families. As cities grew, many African Americans found themselves living among networks of friends or kin but outside a formal nuclear family structure (husband, wife, and their children). Besides the nature of employment that took them away from their families, many city dwellers were single men and women who had come to the city from the country seeking work. People who were poorly paid in their jobs, or who could not find work, or were turned away because of prejudice, waited longer to

Scholar W. E. B. Du Bois, the first African American to earn a Ph.D. at Harvard, interviewed hundreds of black residents of Philadelphia for his landmark study, The Philadelphia Negro, *published in 1897.*

marry. As a result, African Americans in the cities remained single later than those in the country and began having children when they were older. Among the poorest black urban residents—people who suffered most from the strains of over-crowded housing, poverty, and crime—relationships might not be formalized and family arrangements might not last. Because of work conditions that fueled the cycle of poverty, black families tended to be smaller in size in the city than in the country; husbands and wives deprived of work, time, or adequate food and housing limited the number of their offspring or delayed having children. In the Northern cities, many more black women than those in the rural South remained childless throughout their lives. Whereas all members of a sharecropping family, old and young, worked in the fields and contributed to the family income, in the city it was the individual adult, rather than the family unit, who was most involved in earning support.

A neighborhood survey conducted in 1896 in Philadelphia found that 57 percent of black women and 48.7 percent of men over the age of 15 were single, widowed, or divorced. These figures included the 85 percent of women over the age of 60 who were either no longer or never married. Black women outnumbered black men in major Southern cities such as Atlanta, New Orleans, Mobile, Richmond, and Savannah. This was true in Philadelphia as well, where an 1896 survey of the black population of the Seventh Ward revealed that there were 1,150 females to every 1,000 males. Of those African Americans who established families, about eight out of ten, in Southern and Northern cities alike, lived in households that were headed by two parents. But about twice as many urban as rural black households were headed by a woman alone.

In 1896–97 the African-American scholar W. E. B. Du Bois interviewed hundreds of black residents about their families in a house-to-house study he conducted with the help of Isabel Eaton in Philadelphia. Their findings were published in a book called *The Philadelphia Negro*. In addition to noting "an abnormal excess of females" among the black people in Philadelphia, Du Bois reported that an African-American "woman has but three careers open to her in this city: domestic service, sewing, or married life." Staying home from work to make married life a woman's "career," although it might have been desired by working-class couples, was mostly just an option for the middle class. While white women of all classes viewed marriage as an alternative to employment, and most endeavored to stop working outside the home when they married, this was not true for black women. Many black women worked for pay throughout their life spans, in spite of marriage, childraising, and old age.

Residential segregation meant that African Americans were excluded from living in the nicer sections of cities, which were occupied by whites, and were crowded into neighborhoods that had become defined as black. In Washington, D.C., blacks lived in brick or wooden-framed houses in alleyways, built in the middle of blocks behind more stately buildings fronting the main streets and occupied by whites.

In other cities, including Boston and Philadelphia, the backyards of existing buildings were filled with new tenements to accommodate the great need for housing. Theft, violence, and vice were part of black city life, and became more so in the 1890s as black young people who were raised by working parents with little means could often find no jobs for themselves and were welcomed into a developing criminal subculture. Illness also had its impact on black families. Becoming seriously ill was a constant threat for poor city dwellers, who lived in conditions of malnourishment, poor ventilation, and lack of heating in which infectious disease could flourish.

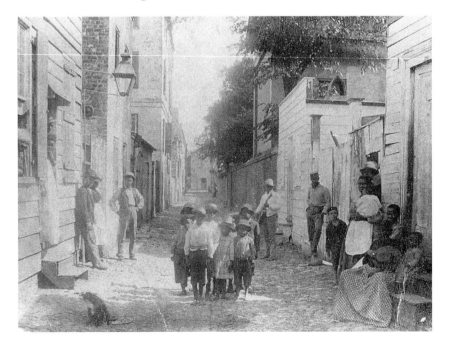

A black section of Charleston, South Carolina, about 1880. Racism and poverty produced tightly packed housing conditions, and wooden buildings built on alleyways were home to many African Americans who lived in cities in both the North and the South.

Pay for all African Americans was low. Black men were paid at lower rates than white men or women for equivalent work, and black women made less than black men. In Philadelphia in the late 1890s, according to the Du Bois study, a black man working as a cementer reported that he "receives $1.75 a day; white workmen get $2-$3." Another man "worked for a firm as china packer, and they said he was the best packer they had. He, however, received but $6 a week while the white packers received $12."

At the same time that pay was lower, rent for African Americans was higher than that paid by whites for the same accommodations. Black Philadelphians living on one street in 1896 reported that African Americans paid "$12 to $14 and the whites $9 and $10. The houses are all alike." A black family moving into a house was charged "$13 a month where the preceding white family had paid $10."

Skin color made a difference in employment. Lighter-skinned women and men of mixed-race heritage were more likely than blacks to be middle-class or wealthy, to have inheritances, own property, have acquired skills through education, be involved in the leadership of organizations, and work in professional or entrepreneurial capacities. Clergy, teaching, medicine, and the law were the most common professional occupations among middle-class African Americans in the city. Still, because of the racial prejudice of whites, a majority of mulatto people were restricted to the same narrow range of occupations and opportunities as their darker-skinned sisters and brothers. The bottom level of urban employment was filled with literate and capable African-American men and women who had skills and abilities they were not allowed to use in the workforce and who were vastly overqualified for the work that they were hired to do.

African Americans did many things to counteract job discrimination and to overcome the isolation and family problems that were the social side effects of that form of prejudice. Social status among blacks in cities came from other sources besides a person's occupation. As in the country, women who moved to towns and cities often took up residence near kin and friends, so that their household existed not in isolation but in a network of others. They also boarded in the homes of siblings, cousins, or acquaintances, or took in boarders themselves. Black benevolent societies, mutual aid associations, fraternal orders, and church auxiliaries also thrived in the cities, with women's groups very active among them. In places like Petersburg, Virginia, and Atlanta, Georgia, in the 1890s black women's volunteer groups such as the Ladies Union, the Ladies Working Club, the

Daughters of Zion, the Sisters of Love, and the Sisters of Rebeccah provided help in the form of food, clothing, medical care, and assistance with funeral arrangements to working women and families in need. They also functioned as social clubs, bringing community activists and neighbors together for fun and friendship. Like these associations, black churches combined social welfare functions and opportunities for socializing. In addition to providing services such as food kitchens and informal employment bureaus, they were key centers for mass meetings and political debates, spiritual renewal, and shared expressions of faith.

The self-reliance and loyalties that were fostered by these group aspects of urban life were also reinforced by the choices that black men and women made about their labor. Although white employers in the cities wanted black women to supply the domestic labor that was necessary to maintain white households (much as white rural landlords wanted black sharecropper families to work the land for white profit), black women preferred the greater autonomy that they had working as independent laundresses instead of as household servants. As isolated live-in maids and

Members of a black church on a picnic. Churches offered a host of services to urban blacks, from providing food and clothing to the needy to offering opportunities to socialize.

cooks, they rarely saw their own children and were never far from their white employer's beck and call. As one anonymous woman described her own household service experience in the *Atlanta Independent*, "I am the slave, body and soul, of this family." By working in white households but living in their own homes, or taking in washing and ironing and staying at home, domestic workers and laundresses were able to give more time to their own families and social networks, and to be more centrally involved as members and activists in their churches and communities. Some laundry workers strengthened their position by forming Washing Society collectives, which were benevolent aid networks of washerwomen.

The Atlanta washerwomen's strike of 1881 is an example of the successful statement black working women could make by standing together. White city boosters in Atlanta organized an International Cotton Exposition to celebrate the New South's embrace of industrialism and Northern capital investment. The washerwomen, meanwhile, spread the word through church congregations that a mass meeting would be held at a certain church, and in July 1881 they met and formed a Washing Society. On July 19 they went out on strike, demanding higher wages to be paid to all members at a standard rate.

The white city council threatened to levy a business tax against the women workers, and landlords punished strikers who were their tenants by raising rents. The August 3, 1881, edition of the *Atlanta Constitution* reported that the strikers countered by announcing that they were willing to pay fees to the city "as a protection so we can control the washing for the city." They also told the council members to make up their minds soon: "We mean business this week or no washing." The influence of the initial mass meeting at the church continued to grow wider, as household workers, asking for higher wages, walked off their jobs and black male waiters at a prominent Atlanta hotel refused service to the dining room until their wages were raised.

In addition to doing service and trade work in the cities, African Americans worked in industries. Sometimes families that were primarily from the country would combine farming with seasonal industrial work. When men would go away for part of a year to work for wages, the women and young people in the family would remain behind to work the farm. Different sorts of wage work were available. In Florida in the 1890s, for example, more than 100,000 black men worked in the forestry industry, felling trees.

Sometimes the pattern of leaving and staying among men and women was reversed: for families who lived along the Atlantic coast, it was often the women, rather than the men, who would leave home to find seasonal work in seafood processing plants. In rare instances, women would do jobs usually done by men, stepping in, for example, when a husband or brother was unable to work and filling his place in earning wages for the family in industry or manual labor. This kind of fill-in labor done by women has been celebrated in the verse of a song about John Henry, a legendary African-American man who worked laying steel rails for the railroads. The verse went like this when the folksinger Leadbelly (who was born in Louisiana in 1888 and whose real name was Huddie Leadbetter) sang it:

> John Henry had a little woman, her name was sweet Polly Ann.
> John Henry taken sick, boy, had to go to bed,
> Polly Ann drove steel like a man,
> Lord, Lord, Polly Ann drove steel like a man.
> Polly Ann drove steel like a man,
> Lord, Lord, Polly Ann drove steel like a man.

Not all labor that African Americans did was voluntary. The convict lease system, in which prison officials collected fees from private employers

While the majority of African-American women found employment as laundresses or in domestic service, a growing number were employed in industry, including those who removed stems and sorted leaves in tobacco processing plants.

Renting out black convicts to private employers was a lucrative source of income for many Southern states. Harsh laws that unfairly targeted blacks ensured a steady supply of convicts and a steady stream of revenue for the state.

who contracted with the state for work done by prisoners outside prison facilities, was a source of revenue for the penitentiaries and states that allowed the practice. It also provided industrialists with a steady labor supply otherwise unavailable in the South, where a majority of white as well as black workers were trained in agriculture rather than industry and were used to seasonal or part-time patterns of working.

Laws called Black Codes made black people susceptible to arrest for petty crimes and, once imprisoned, made them available to be assigned to do forced labor. Under these laws, for example, black men who were homeless or unemployed could be arrested by whites and imprisoned on charges of vagrancy or loitering. Once convicted of a crime, they could be made to work under guard for the duration of their prison term rather than spend the time inside a penitentiary or jail.

The states of Alabama, Georgia, and Tennessee all had convict lease systems, and the brunt of the system was borne by African Americans. Eighty to ninety percent of all inmates in Alabama in the 1880s and 1890s were black. In Tennessee, more than 60 percent of the prison population was black, and black convicts made up more than 70 percent of those who were leased out to work in coal mines. Between October 1888 and September 1889, 26 convicts died from injuries suffered in the Dade Coal Company mine in Georgia. Others were flogged for rebelling, and two men were shot trying to escape.

In 1891 labor activists in eastern Tennessee challenged the policies of the Tennessee Coal and Iron Company, which was by that time one of the major employers of convict labor in the state. In July 1891 hundreds of miners held a mass meeting. After the gathering they began a series of actions in which they armed themselves and took control of convict camps, freeing the men who were held within them. In the first such action, they freed convicts who were being sent to work in the company's Briceville mine and put them on trains headed for Knoxville or Nashville. Most of the liberated prisoners were black. More than 100 of them were able to escape, but most were eventually recaptured and returned to prison.

The free laborers were furious that the mining company planned to replace them with less expensive convict workers whose labor they could better control. One observer of the rebellion of the free laborers, H. H. Schwartz, reported in the *United Mine Workers Journal* that "whites and Negroes are standing shoulder to shoulder" in the actions. Their protest sparked surprise investigations of the mines, during which the investigators found many safety and health violations. It also forced the Tennessee State Legislature to hold a special session to reconsider use of the convict labor system. When the legislators decided to continue the system because of the money it made for the state and the contracting companies, the scattered protests became an organized uprising. Support for the Tennessee protestors spread among miners in Kentucky and Virginia. In August 1892 the convict camp at Tracy City, Tennessee, was burned to the ground by protesting miners, and the inmates set free. Hundreds of miners were imprisoned by state militia that had been called out to subdue the protesters, and Jake Witsen, a black miner who was a leader of the free laborers' actions, was shot to death by soldiers. Thousands of opponents of the convict lease system attended his funeral in respect for his leadership and to bring public notice to the injustice of his death. As a result, in 1893 the Tennessee legislature passed a bill abolishing convict leasing as of January 1896, which is when the Tennessee Iron and Coal Company's contract with the state ended.

Several of the activists who led the convict wars in eastern Tennessee were involved in the Knights of Labor or in the United Mine Workers of America. The United Mine Workers was formed in 1890 during a time when mining was expanding as an area of employment for African Americans. By the turn of the century, some 10 to 15 percent of the 400,000 people working in mines were African Americans. They worked mainly in areas bordering between the North and the South (West Virginia, Kentucky, Tennessee) and in Alabama. In the 1890s some of them also came to work in mines further north—in places like Ohio, Illinois, or Pennsylvania—as did immigrants from eastern and southern Europe, who joined the Irish immigrants and native-born whites who had previously

Miners and their families in Lexington, Kentucky. In the late 19th century, many African-American men worked in mines in states like Kentucky and West Virginia, and, increasingly, in the North.

made up most of the workforces in the mines. In addition to racial and cultural differences, there were religious differences between native-born blacks and whites and the newer immigrants. Instead of organizing these different groups of miners separately, the United Mine Workers attempted to join members of different backgrounds into what were called "mixed" locals. African Americans were an important part of building the union, and by 1900 20,000 black miners belonged to it.

Richard L. Davis was a black organizer in Ohio. He was one of the founders of the United Mine Workers and became a national leader of the union. He was born in Virginia at the end of the Civil War and had begun working in a tobacco factory in Roanoake when he was eight years old. At age 17 he became a coal miner and went to work first in West Virginia and then in Ohio, where he married and had a family. He and other workers in the town of Rendville, Ohio, faced long periods of unemployment in the mid-1890s, when an economic depression caused many of the mines in Ohio to shut down or operate on irregular schedules. "No work and much destitution," Davis wrote of their condition in 1895 in one of several long, articulate letters to the *United Mine Workers Journal* about mining towns and unionization in the 1890s.

A powerful speaker, he was elected to the national executive board of the United Mine Workers in 1896 and again in 1897. He often used verses from the Bible and examples of things that his fellow workers knew well from church to explain the importance of standing together to try to win greater rights and to look for justice in this world as well as in heaven. "I know that in former days you used to sing 'Give me Jesus, give me Jesus, you may have all the world, just give me Jesus,'" he told his audience of miners in a letter to the *United Mine Workers Journal* on April 18, 1892. "But the day has now come that we want a little money along with our Jesus, so we want to change that old song and ask for a little of the world as well. Don't you think so, friends?"

Davis was involved in the Knights of Labor as well as in the United Mine Workers. The Knights of Labor was organized in 1869 and reached the height of its influence in 1886, when more than 700,000 members belonged. The membership included between 60,000 and 90,000 black people, who, like Davis, joined through the locals in their communities. But unlike most traditional unions or the United Mine Workers, which focused on skilled workers or those in a particular trade, the Knights of Labor welcomed all kinds of laborers: farmers, field workers, women, men, black and white crafts workers, and those employed in all kinds of jobs in different industries.

African Americans like Davis were among the organizers who went into neighborhoods, churches, and workplaces to encourage other laborers to join. Many who became involved in the Knights of Labor did so for idealistic reasons. They believed, as Davis wrote in a letter to the mine workers' journal, in the "brotherhood of all mankind no matter what the color of his skin may be" and in the inherent equality of black and white people. Organizers like Davis who believed in these values established a tradition of interracial unionism among lumber workers in Florida, coal miners in Birmingham, Alabama, freight handlers in Galveston, Texas, and male and female tobacco workers in Richmond, Virginia.

Although many white members of the Knights opposed the organization of black workers, the Knights took steps to defy public practices that denied social equality to blacks. In October 1886, for example, they held a convention in Richmond, Virginia, at which a black delegate named Frank Ferrell, who was from New York, spoke to the assembly along with white dignitaries. He did so in defiance of local custom, which barred black people from sitting with whites in public places or from speaking to audiences made up primarily of whites.

Three workers in Onslow County, North Carolina. In the late 19th century black workers sought to advance beyond manual labor to jobs in manufacturing, mining, and industry, and self-employment in crafts.

Terence V. Powderly, the head of the Knights, believed that white and black workers doing the same kind of work should have equal wages. He also noted that one of the goals of the Knights was to provide education to working-class children, not just to those of the middle and upper classes. In a speech to an assembly in Richmond, Virginia, in January 1885, he explained that in the places where the Knights had become established the "colored men are advocating the holding of free night schools for the children of black and white. . . . The politicians have kept the white and black [working] men of the South apart, while crushing both. Our aim shall be to educate both and elevate them by bringing them together."

A black member of the Knights in Fort Worth, Texas, wrote to Powderly on October 15, 1886, to tell him that his position "on the color line question meets the approval of the colored people in this part of the south and this part of the state." He added that he had "been a faithful member" of the organization "since June 28th 85 [and] I am highly pleased with its principles."

For many working-class African Americans, participation in Knights of Labor activities was one way of being treated with the kind of respect that was afforded mainly to middle-class people, and to the working class within their own churches and secret societies. This was especially true for the women. The African-American journalist Ida B. Wells reported on a meeting of the Knights of Labor that she attended in a piece published the January 22, 1887, issue of the *Cleveland Gazette*. "I noticed that everyone who came was welcomed and every woman from black to white was seated

Despite the opposition of many white members of the Knights of Labor, Frank M. Ferrell, a black delegate from New York, addressed a meeting of the Knights in 1886.

with courtesy usually extended to white ladies alone in this town," Wells observed. "It was the first assembly of the sort in this town where color was not the criterion to recognition as ladies and gentlemen."

The Knights of Labor also tried to use collective actions to better working conditions. In Louisiana the year after Frank Ferrell spoke in Richmond, some 6,000 to 10,000 laborers, mostly black, walked off their jobs in the sugarcane fields in support of a Knights of Labor strike for higher wages. Like the mine workers who participated in the convict wars in

Tennessee, they faced white violence as a consequence of their demands, and several black strikers were killed when companies of state militia were sent in to end the strike.

In Richmond, black and white Knights led their families and neighbors in supporting a mass consumer boycott in 1885. They refused to buy goods that had been made with convict labor. Mechanization was another issue that concerned Knights who worked in factories. In tobacco factories, for example, the automatic lump machine was introduced in the early 1880s. It combined the tasks and speeded the work previously done manually by various men and women who had sorted and then pressed leaves of tobacco into lumps of standardized sizes and weights to await further processing. Work became more regimented and the men and women in the factories had less control over the pace and style of their work flow. Others found their skills outmoded. In response to these changes, some Knights planned to open a series of cooperatively run tobacco factories.

In Richmond, where the Knights organized a large portion of the tobacco workforce, Richard Thompson, one of the local leaders of the Knights in 1886, was a skilled lumpmaker in a tobacco factory. Thompson came from an activist family that had been involved in benevolent associations, including one that worked to establish a reading room, or small library, for poor residents in the city. He was a member of the First African Baptist Church, was married, and had four children. He and his wife Adelaide lived in a tenement building that housed two other families. It was located near his parents' home in a neighborhood where almost everyone was black and employed in the tobacco industry. Thompson was the son of a carpenter. Another Knights leader, Joseph Burwell, was a barber who also had family connections to the First African Baptist Church and black secret societies. A third, William Fields, was the son of a washerwoman. He began working in the factories when he was a teenager. For these men, like other African Americans who became involved in the Knights, the labor movement was one part of their deep involvement in their working-class neighborhood, an extension of their family's history of work and social connections, and a means of expression for their belief in equal rights and racial pride.

African-American workers also had success organizing in New Orleans, where in 1880 black and white dockworkers who pressed, moved, and shipped bales of cotton on the Mississippi River wharves formed a labor coalition called the Cotton Men's Executive Council. The council

Blacks at work in a tobacco factory. Both women and men were hired to process tobacco, but they usually were assigned to different kinds of tasks. In places like Richmond, Virginia, some black tobacco workers were active in the Knights of Labor.

coordinated the goals of several dock unions, and covered common laborers as well as men working in the trades. Prior to the formation of the council, black cotton rollers, teamsters, coopers, wheelers, and freight handlers had already created their own separate benevolent or mutual aid associations similar to the Washing Society that black washerwomen had formed in Atlanta. They met together to set uniform wages for their specialties and to help each other in times of need. Demands of the unions involved in the council, which represented some 15,000 workers, centered around the need for higher wages. In September 1880 black unionists joined whites in their same industries in a series of strikes that brought wage increases for teamsters, loaders, and other dockworkers.

A year later the unionized waterfront workers struck again, asking for fair wages and for the employers to recognize the union as the representative of the workers. Black unionists kept order until the second week of the general dock strike, when a lone policeman attempted to arrest a black teamster on a city street. The teamster, James Hawkins, was a person that the September 1881 *Weekly Louisianian* described as a "law abiding, peaceful man." He proclaimed his innocence when approached by the policeman and resisted the arrest. The policeman's actions drew the ire of the local African-American women, who threw frying pans and utensils at him from their windows. In the resulting commotion, the police officer drew his gun and shot Hawkins twice, killing him.

Hawkins was murdered, as one of the *Weekly Louisianian* reports of the killing put it, "for no other cause than that a negro has no rights which a police officer is bound to respect." Hawkins's death galvanized the working-class neighborhood. Infuriated black and white women emerged from their houses and crowded around Hawkins's bloody body, shouting angrily at the police officers who had gathered. Black men drew together in groups and marched to the intersection where the shooting had occurred. Residents of the neighborhood, including women and children, ran over and put nearby dock work being done by strikebreakers to a stop. Popular resistance in support of the strikers grew as the news spread from neighbor to friend about what had happened to Hawkins. With his unjust death, the strike had become the whole community's business.

White unionists joined black dockworkers and their families at Hawkins's funeral, and they emerged determined to defy the powers that would deny them a better standard of living and their desire to have a say in the structure of their own work. They shut down work on the riverfront. Soon all parties involved in the strike met and negotiated a settlement. The strikers succeeded in winning the employers' agreement to standard wages on the docks for each category of labor and some protections for the unions in hiring. More importantly, they set a standard for biracial working-class unionism that lasted in New Orleans into the 1890s.

The closely related populist and agrarian movements of the 1890s were other ways in which black workers sought to organize both among themselves and, for greater strength, with white working people. Their goals were the defense of racial justice and economic equity in American society. Populism and small farmers' associations were part of a grassroots political movement whose supporters sought to form alliances between poor and working people, especially those who made their living in agriculture.

For example, black farmers in Lovejoy, Texas, formed the Colored Farmers' National Alliance and Cooperative Union in March 1888. Their membership expanded and they joined with white farmers' groups from the Midwest and South. By 1891 the alliance had more than 1 million members in 12 states. Like the Knights of Labor, the farmers' alliances supported the idea of workers' cooperatives, enterprises in which workers would pool their resources, exchange labor or contribute goods, and share profits. They also wanted to reform wage work to give working people better payment for their labor, and they organized boycotts of merchants who engaged in unfair practices. They sponsored consumer cooperative stores in Southern cities, helped members who were struggling to pay mortgages on their land, and worked to improve the education provided to rural black children.

While the farmers' alliances were being formed, the Populist or People's Party emerged as an independent political party in February 1892, when farmers, labor unionists, and reformers met in St. Louis to develop a program to challenge business interests and the low prices being paid for agricultural goods. Populists supported the rights of nonlandowning laborers, including black tenant farmers and field workers, and wanted reform of the country's financial system.

In some areas, one of the party's strategies for change was to try to elect black officials to public office. These officials, it was hoped, would be committed to black civil and political rights, including an end to convict lease systems, the right of black people to serve on juries, and what one black delegate from the Colored Farmers' Alliance termed a "free vote and an honest count."

This strategy had some success in North Carolina, where 10 black candidates were elected to the state legislature on Populist-Republican tickets in the 1890s, and many more gained county and municipal offices. Racism as well as class differences marred the progressive aspects of the Populist cause over time, as white small farmers who owned land saw their own interests diverge from those of black sharecroppers and tenant farmers who did not own property.

Farmers hauling their crop to market. In the 1890s African-American farmers formed collectives, supported the Populist party, and worked in conjunction with farmers' organizations in an effort to improve their lot.

There were many successes in black-white working people's cooperation in farmers' alliances, populist political coalitions, the Knights of Labor, and among unionists such as the miners in Tennessee and the dockworkers in Louisiana. But one of the unresolved questions in black industrial workers' minds at the end of the 1800s was whether it was better to compete against free white labor for jobs or to join in coalition with white workers to collectively demand better wages and conditions. Skepticism about the genuineness of whites' desire for long-range cooperation was rampant. As John Lucus Dennis, a black worker at the Black Diamond Steel Works in Pittsburgh, put it in a letter to the *New York Freeman*: "Our experience as a race with these organizations has, on the whole, not been such as to give us either great satisfaction or confidence in white men's fidelity."

Mining and work in the cities were two areas where the dilemma between competition or attempted coalition continually played out. In the North, mine workers in the late 1800s were almost all white. Mine operators' use of Southern black workers as strikebreakers thus took on more directly racial meanings than it did in the South, where blacks found themselves on both the unemployed and free labor sides of such conflicts. In both the North and the South, industrialists used racial differences to divide the work force and prevent unionization. They paid black workers less money than white workers for the same labor, and they denied the higher-paid and higher-status positions in industries to blacks. Organized labor often followed these kinds of prejudiced policies. White union members often prevented blacks from becoming apprentices in trades or members of unions, and even unions that claimed biracial principles were dominated by white leadership and weakened by segregated practices, including the organization of separate locals for whites and blacks. African-American experience in unions varied a great deal from industry to industry and from one region or local to another. It also varied in the same places over time: a successful action in which white and black union members rallied together could be an exceptional event. A long history of exclusion and discrimination might precede and or follow the period of cooperation. Many black workers were alienated from the very idea of involvement in organized labor because of their association of labor activism with white working-class racism and with union opposition to black industrial employment. At least 50 strikes took place in American industries between 1880 and 1900 in which white workers opposed the hiring of blacks.

Blacks who worked in crafts like carpentry, woodworking, or bricklaying were among those who suffered from white policies of exclusion. This was one reason why the number of black artisans and crafts workers that had once seemed so prevalent in the cities declined, and black men were gradually moved more and more into unskilled areas of labor. Although Henry W. Grady said in his 1890 book, *The New South*, that in Atlanta "white and black carpenters and masons work together on the same buildings, white and black shoemakers and mechanics in the same shops. White and black hackmen drive on the same streets," things were not always so harmonious. Many whites in the building trades did not welcome black carpenters and joiners into their unions, for example, and white bricklayers hired in the cities were known to walk off the job rather than work beside black brickmasons.

This kind of experience could occur whether or not a union was involved. Nonunion white women spinners and weavers in textile factories often spurned working with newly hired black women. Workers who did not have a trade or do skilled work were often excluded from union eligibility of any kind, since craft unions—such as those that represented conductors, locomotive firemen, or engineers in the railway industry—did not accept unskilled or semiskilled workers into their membership.

Black workers also sometimes found themselves in a tug-of-war between industrialists and the unions. In 1890 a leaflet was circulated among black miners in Birmingham, Alabama, that stated "WANTED! COLORED coal-miners for Weir City, Kan., district, the paradise of col-

The members of a carpenters' union in Jacksonville, Florida. Blacks who worked in crafts such as carpentry or bricklaying often faced strong opposition from their white counterparts.

ored people. . . . Special train will leave Birmingham the 13th. Transportation advanced. Get ready and go to the land of promise." When the black miners who responded to this call arrived in Kansas, they found the white workers at the mines on strike and manning a stockade barring the entrance to the work site. Some joined the strikers; others returned home to Alabama when the union paid their way. Still others seized the opportunity for employment at higher wages than they earned in Birmingham, but under conditions that hardly constituted a paradise for black people.

What was happening in the places that people worked mirrored the changes that had slowly been occurring on the political front since the end of the political Reconstruction that followed the Civil War. The exclusion from skilled and better paying jobs and from union representation that African Americans were experiencing in the workplace coincided with the loss of rights to vote, to be elected to office, to live where one chose, or to receive the kind of education that black parents wanted for their children. Miner and labor organizer Richard L. Davis wrote to the *United Mine Workers' Journal* on May 25, 1893, to say that the solution to the so-called "race problem, or what ought or should be done with the negro," seemed "plainly evident" to him. The African-American person, Davis wrote, "is a citizen of this country and should be treated as such." The opposite kind of treatment, however, was occurring. Political privileges and the rights of citizenship were being taken away, and violence and denial of opportunity were things with which African Americans increasingly had to contend.

CHAPTER 3

JUSTICE: "THEY HAVE PROMISED US LAW . . . AND GIVEN US VIOLENCE"

> Where human life is insecure through either weakness or viciousness in the administration of law, there must be a lack of justice and where this is wanting, nothing can make up the deficiency.
> —Frances Ellen Watkins Harper, speaking to the National Council of Women, Washington, D.C., February 22, 1891

> Tell my people . . . There is no justice for them here.
> —Thomas Moss to his abductors, moments before being lynched on the outskirts of Memphis, Tennessee, March 9, 1892

I t was a spring day in May 1884. A young, well-dressed school-teacher named Ida B. Wells refused to comply with a conductor's request that she move from the first-class "ladies'" section of a Chesapeake, Ohio, and Southwestern Railroad train to a second-class smoking car further back in the train. Ida B. Wells was 21 years old. She often took the 10-mile train trip between Memphis, Tennessee, where she lived, and the town of Woodstock, where she taught public school.

But this day was different. On this day the conductor who came to take her ticket tried to enforce a Jim Crow law that had been passed in Tennessee two years before, authorizing separate accommodations for black and white travelers. When the conductor asked her to change cars, Wells protested. Then the conductor tried to pull her from her seat. Soon the two of them were scuffling in the aisle of the ladies' car as he tried to force her off the train and she attempted to keep her seat. Two other railroad employees came running to aid the conductor, and Wells was dragged away, resisting, and removed from the train, which was stopped in a station at the time the incident took place. When Wells chose to resist the trainmen, she

These three men were lynched near Forge, Virginia, in 1891.

turned a corner in her life. She began what would become a lifetime of public activism in which she would use words and deeds to challenge the injustices the American legal system dealt to African Americans.

On that May day she did not stop with standing up for herself inside the train. When she got home after the incident, she sought out a lawyer and filed a lawsuit against the railroad. Legal victory was briefly hers. The judge who heard the case in the local circuit court in December 1884 ruled in her favor. Although he did not question the policy of segregation itself, he found that the smoking car did not constitute accommodations equal to those of the first-class passenger car, and that Wells, having paid for a first-class ticket, deserved first-class conditions of travel. The railroad appealed his judgment, however, and at the beginning of April 1887 the Tennessee Supreme Court reversed the lower court's ruling.

"I felt so disappointed," Ida B. Wells wrote in her diary on April 5, 1887, describing how she reacted to the news of the high court decision. She went on to explain what she had wanted to accomplish by filing the case. "I had hoped such great things from my suit for my people generally. I have firmly believed all along that the law was on our side and would, when we appealed to it, give us justice." She then voiced her disillusionment in discovering that this ideal was not supported. "I feel shorn of that belief and utterly discouraged," she confessed to her diary, "and just now, if it were possible, would gather my race in my arms and fly away with them." "O God," she continued, "is there no redress, no peace, no justice in this land for us?"

Ida B. Wells's act of defiance in the cause of equal justice aboard the Chesapeake, Ohio, and Southwestern Railroad and her decision to bring the issue before the Tennessee courts made her a key part of the African-American challenge to a larger legal process that was occurring throughout the 1880s and 1890s. During this time American laws that had

In 1884, Ida B. Wells challenged a Tennessee law authorizing separate accommodations for blacks and whites while on trains. A local judge ruled in her favor, but the Tennessee Supreme Court ultimately reversed the lower court's ruling.

been created in the Reconstruction era to guarantee the extension of rights to former slaves were reinterpreted by state and federal courts. As a result, the standard of justice by which black and white citizens lived was altered for decades to come.

These changes in rights came in two important areas. One was in a series of laws and court rulings about the right of blacks to equal access to public places such as inns, restaurants, parks, and—perhaps most importantly—schools, as well as the ability to travel in the same way as whites on trains, ships, and streetcars. These legal actions raised questions about how the principle of equality should be understood, and also how that principle should be justly applied to society. Most specifically, they created a legal debate about racial integration versus segregation.

The second area where legislation and court cases changed the meaning of racial justice was in regard to political or citizenship rights. In the last decades of the 19th century, states began to pass measures that resulted in the loss of political participation by African Americans. The loss of Reconstruction-era protections of the right of African-American men to vote influenced other rights as well, including the ability of blacks to be elected to political office, participate in political parties, and serve on juries. This last loss was doubly harmful, because the exclusion of African Americans from juries interfered with the right of black defendants to have

Freed slaves line up to vote in New Orleans shortly after the end of the Civil War. Access to the ballot box soon ended for the majority of blacks as states began passing laws limiting the ability of African Americans to vote.

their cases heard by juries of their peers—to be judged, according to the law, by people like themselves.

The most terrible outcome of this erosion of rights was the denial of due process of law, either in the failure to arrest or prosecute people who committed crimes against African Americans, or the assurance of fair apprehension and trial of African Americans who were accused of wrongdoing. In the years when statutes were going into effect limiting black people's social and political rights, violence was often directed at African-American citizens. Black men and women were hurt or killed without being tried for alleged misdoings, and the white people who committed atrocities against blacks were not penalized for them. Often the misdeeds for which African Americans were punished outside the law was the simple "crime" of success itself.

Ida B. Wells's case against the railroad fit squarely into the first area in which African-American rights were denied. Her suit was one of the important legal tests by African Americans of rulings made by the U.S. Supreme Court in *Civil Rights Cases* (1883). And her refusal to give up her seat on the train and the lawsuit that stemmed from her action foreshadowed a similar protest that a man named Homer A. Plessy would begin aboard a train in Louisiana in 1890.

Plessy's case, which was heard by the U.S. Supreme Court in 1896, would set the legal precedent, or standard by which other similar cases would be judged, that made it possible for states to continue to enforce racial segregation laws and practices. Jim Crow laws created between the 1870s and 1910 would remain in force for decades. They would not be overthrown until a successful legal campaign by a new generation of African-American activists led to the U.S. Supreme Court's 1954 ruling in *Brown* v. *Board of Education* and to the civil rights movement that followed it.

In filing her suit to protest the railroad's attempt to segregate its passenger cars by race, Wells became the first African American to challenge the U.S. Supreme Court ruling of 1883 that denied access to blacks to transportation, theaters, hotels, or other places regularly used by the public. That case had revolved around the meaning of the 14th Amendment to the U.S. Constitution, which guaranteed that no state could make discriminatory laws or "deprive any person of life, liberty, or property without due process of law, nor deny to any person within its jurisdiction the equal protection of the laws." The justices ruled that this amendment was not meant to be applied to what they called "private wrongs," or the experience of discrimination by individual persons on private property. (The justices included in their definition of such property privately owned theaters, trains, and hotels.)

African-American journalists and politicians were in the forefront of the public outcry against the legal decisions and state laws that endorsed segregation. The newspaper writers and editors who gathered at the Afro-American Press Convention of 1890 denounced the consignment of black people to second-class facilities aboard railroads. Black members of the state legislatures in Louisiana and Arkansas fought against the segregation bills that were introduced in their legislative bodies in 1890 and 1891. Resistance also continued among African-American citizens' groups in cities and towns around the nation.

In Atlanta, Georgia, in 1892 a group of black citizens organized a successful boycott of the city's streetcars after the city council ordered separate cars for white and black passengers. Similar public demonstrations and boycott actions took place in Augusta, Georgia, in 1898, and in Savannah, Georgia, in 1899.

Homer A. Plessy was one of the countless number of African-American activists in cities North and South. The case that carried his name, *Plessy* v. *Ferguson*, was heard in the courts as the result of organized local African-American opposition to the Louisiana Separate Car Act of 1890. The new Louisiana law required what was termed "equal but separate" accommodations for white and nonwhite passengers on railways, with seats to be assigned in segregated cars according to race. In practice, these separate-but-equal regulations actually resulted in segregated and unequal treatment, with whites receiving the best accommodations or services available and blacks given inferior accommodations. On the trains, for example, there were no cars for blacks that were the equivalent of the first-class passenger cars. No matter what kind of ticket they could afford, African Americans from all walks of life were seated together in so-called smoking cars, where seating was less comfortable and smoking was allowed. According to the Louisiana law, passengers who refused to comply with the rules of segregation could be removed from trains and were permitted no legal recourse.

African-American members of the American Citizens' Equal Rights Association in New Orleans reacted immediately to the threat of the separate cars bill. They filed a memorial with the Louisiana legislature on May 24, 1890, protesting that the measure violated the principle that all citizens are created equal before the law. The leaders of the protest action were Dr. Louis A. Martinet, a lawyer and physician who owned the *New Orleans Crusader,* and Rodolphe L. Desdunes, a customs clerk. Both men were prominent middle-class members of New Orleans's mixed-race creole community. They used the *Crusader* as a forum to attack the separate car act and called for cases to be brought to the courts that would test the constitutionality of the new legislation.

The first major test case was instigated by Homer A. Plessy, a 34-year-old friend of the Desdunes family, who was also a light-skinned member of the elite New Orleans creole community. Plessy was arrested soon after he boarded the East Louisiana Railway on June 7, 1892, and sat down in the coach set aside for whites.

The results, as in Ida B. Wells's case, were not what the African-American activists who planned the test case had sought. Instead of upholding the rights of equity and federal protection guaranteed by the 14th Amendment, as the Citizens Committee activists had hoped, the court in effect dismantled the authority of the amendment's equal protection clause and instead ruled that separation of races on railways was valid. The court also ruled that the passage of separate-but-equal Jim Crow laws was an appropriate and reasonable exercise of state legislative authority. The court thus provided the constitutional basis by which Southern states could enforce the practice of racial segregation.

It was not only the 14th Amendment but the 15th that came under fire by white supremacists in the 1880s and 1890s. The 15th Amendment to the U.S. Constitution guaranteed that the "right of citizens of the United States to vote shall not be denied or abridged by the United States, or by any State, on account of race, color, or previous condition of servitude." Beginning with Mississippi in 1890, South Carolina in 1895, Louisiana in 1898, and North Carolina in 1900, and Alabama and Virginia shortly after the turn of the century, several states amended their constitutions with the intention of denying blacks the right to vote. In other states, the legislatures passed laws that were similarly designed to eliminate black voting. These included laws that required people to pass a literacy test, hold property, or reside on the same property for long periods of time in order to register to vote.

Justice Henry Billings Brown wrote the opinion for the U.S. Supreme Court in Plessy v. Ferguson *in 1896 that states could provide "separate but equal" facilities for blacks. The decision was used to justify segregation in many states for more than 50 years.*

Justice John Marshall Harlan was the lone voice of dissent in Plessy v. Ferguson. *He wrote, "In the eye of the law there is in this country no superior, dominant, ruling class of citizens. . . . Our Constitution is color-blind and neither knows nor tolerates classes among citizens."*

Literacy tests discriminated against all people who were not middle-class or wealthy and who thus did not have the benefit of education. But they had a particularly devastating effect on former slaves who had been barred under bondage from learning to read. Residency and property requirements worked against the majority of African Americans in the South, too, because most of them worked as sharecroppers or tenant farmers. They neither owned property nor stayed on the same land from year to year. Poll taxes, or fees that had to be paid in order to be eligible to vote, were among the most effective means of excluding blacks from the ballot box, because African Americans made up a disproportionate number of the poor who could not afford to pay the taxes.

In many Southern states, grandfather clauses stated that anyone whose father or grandfather had been qualified to vote in 1867 did not have to pass literacy or citizenship tests or be subjected to other hurdles to registration. Since the 15th Amendment enfranchising black men was ratified by Congress in 1870, these clauses virtually excluded African Americans, while making it possible for poor whites who might otherwise not be able to pass the tests to vote without having to take them.

What was called the "white primary," or exclusion of blacks from participation in the Democratic party's primaries (pre-election votes by which political parties chose candidates to run for office), also nullified the black vote. That was because the Democratic party so dominated the South by 1900 that whoever was designated as a Democratic candidate was virtually assured of victory in the subsequent election.

These white supremacist measures were effective in taking the vote away from African Americans. The changes they wrought were dramatic. The promises of citizenship for blacks that had been part of the rhetoric of the federal government during the Reconstruction period were undone by state actions and the failure of the federal government to counteract them. The federal government failed to act in part because of racism and in part because of a desire to heal the divisions between the national government and the power of the states, especially the Southern states, that were still ripe from the Civil War. The African-American journalist and activist T. Thomas Fortune analyzed the denial of justice to African Americans and the process of disenfranchisement in his 1884 book *Black and White*. He observed that the exclusion of African Americans from land ownership and voting were the roots of the "great social wrong which has turned the beautiful roses of freedom into thorns to prick the hands of the black men of the South."

Passage of voter restriction laws had a very substantial effect. In Louisiana, where literacy, property, and poll-tax restrictions were enacted, there were 130,344 black registered voters in 1896 and African Americans made up the majority of voters in 26 parishes (districts). By 1900, after these laws were passed, there were only 5,320 black registrants and not one parish had a black majority. By 1904 the number of black registered voters had slipped to 1,342. In Alabama in 1900 there were only 3,000 registered African-American voters, out of a potential pool of almost 150,000 black men who were of voting age.

Corruption and intimidation had preceded the passage of these restrictive laws and helped whites control and limit the black vote. Black support for alternatives to the white supremacist platform of the Southern Democratic party was often suppressed by violence. In Virginia in 1883 there was a white backlash against the Liberal Readjuster party, a coalition of Radical Republicans who had supported black emancipation and postwar Reconstruction, lower-class white farmers, owners of small businesses, and black farmers, sharecroppers, and factory workers that had gained power in the elections of 1879 and voted in progressive reforms that benefited black people.

In Mississippi in 1881 a coalition of Radical Republicans and third-party supporters achieved victories in local elections, including in Copiah County, where more than half of the population was black. Two women testified to a Senate investigative committee about the violence that whites committed in order to put a stop to political attempts to bring about racial justice and reform.

In Danville, Virginia, white conservatives angry at reforms that had taken place since the success of the Liberal Readjuster coalition at the polls in 1879 and 1881 were determined to use the 1883 elections to firmly subordinate African-American residents to white rule. Shortly before election day, November 6, a group of prominent white businessmen issued a circular in the town decrying the idea of black people in positions of authority and claiming that by gaining some political representation, African Americans had become less tractable workers in the white-owned tobacco industry. Blacks were warned not to be on the streets on election day. One conservative proclaimed that the white supremacists would win the election in Danville "votes or no votes" if they had to do it "with double barrel shotguns, breach loading shotguns and Smith and Wesson double-action." White vigilantes took control of the town, forcing campaigning by black and white members of the liberal reform coalition to end. On November 3, they killed three black citizens.

Violet Keeling worked in a tobacco factory in Danville, Virginia, at that time. Investigators from the U.S. Senate asked her whether her husband had voted in the recent 1883 state election. She replied that he had not, and when asked why, she explained that she had been afraid for him to try to cast his ballot, "because life was better to him than the ballot-box, and I thought it was best for him to stay at home and save his life." Mrs. Keeling had stayed home with her husband, afraid that if she ventured out on the streets to go to work that she would be hurt by whites who were bent on controlling the movements of blacks on election day. She reported that there was much talk among the black men she knew about the election, and "it seemed they were all afraid to go to the polls as bad as they wanted to vote, which I believe every colored one there was a Republican and wanted to vote." Some of them had been fired from their jobs just prior to the elections in order to punish them for their political viewpoints, and others were loath to vote for fear of meeting the same fate.

Violet Keeling was unable to vote herself, since the franchise had not yet been extended to women of any race. But she made her own political views clear, and hinted how she would enforce them socially among her neighbors and family members. She stated that if "I knew a colored man that voted the Democratic ticket to come to my house, I would tell him to go somewhere else and visit." When asked how she would react if her husband voted for the white supremacist Democratic ticket, she retorted that she would leave him: "I would just pick up my clothes and go to my father's, if I had a father, or would go to work for 25 cents a day." Elsewhere in Virginia, black residents of towns rallied successfully to ensure their ability to get to the polls. In Petersburg, Virginia, African-Americans organized a parade and guarded the polling places in the city precincts.

While Violet Keeling was afraid for her husband's life if he ventured to the polls in Danville, Selina Wallis experienced Mrs. Keeling's worst fear during election time in Copiah County, Mississippi. She, too, described to Senate investigators what happened in 1883. The Friday before the election

Mrs. Wallis and her husband Thomas were asleep in their bed when they were awakened at about one or two o'clock in the morning by the shouts of men outside their home. Mr. Wallis got out of bed to go to the door, but before he reached it the white vigilantes shoved it open and entered the house. Selina Wallis could see several more men behind them outdoors. They had come on horseback and had guns. They began to question Thomas Wallis and his young adult son, who was also named Thomas. When they took out a rope and attempted to put it around the neck of the younger Thomas Wallis, his father threw up his hand and, calling them gentlemen, asked them to wait. They shot him. As they dragged him out of his house, he was able to take hold of the ax he used for wood cutting, which was lying in its place next to the door. As he tried to defend himself with the ax, several of the men opened fire upon him, and shots ricocheted throughout the house. When the bullets stopped flying, Selina Wallis had been shot in the arm and her husband fatally wounded in the neck. He died almost immediately, collapsing with blood spurting from his neck against his

In 1898 in Wilmington, North Carolina, a white mob swept through the black district of the city, attacking blacks whom they encountered.

wife's skirt. The white men then got on their horses and rode away. They threatened other black people in the neighborhood and in response the neighbors took flight and hid in the woods. The vigilantes were mainly upper-class white men, prominent members of the local planter and business elite, and at the end of October 1883 they had begun making raids against black households whose residents were politically active.

Mob violence and lynching were an effective tool by which conservative whites controlled all kinds of black behavior, not just the effort to exercise citizenship rights, hold political office, or vote. Lynchings most often happened in rural areas and small towns, but mob riots were the creatures of the cities. Violence or the threat of violence was random and widespread. When a black man named Baker was appointed postmaster in the small town of Lake City, South Carolina, in 1898, a white mob surrounded his house and post office in the night and set the building afire, with him and his family members inside. When Mr. and Mrs. Baker and their children attempted to run from the burning house, they were shot on the threshold, Mrs. Baker with her infant in her arms. In the same year that the Bakers died, whites went berserk in Wilmington, North Carolina, at election time and swept through the black district of the city, setting homes and businesses afire and killing and wounding African Americans whom they encountered.

Between 1882 and 1901 more than 100 people were lynched each year, the great majority of them blacks living in Southern states. Almost 2,000 lynchings of African Americans were officially reported in those two decades. Additional murders by lynching occurred, but they went unreported as such in local records and overall statistics. Other attacks were attempted but were successfully fought off by individuals like Jack Trice, who acted in defense of his son when "regulators" like those that had come to the home of Thomas Wallis arrived at the Trice home in Palmetto, outside Jacksonville, Florida, in May 1896. Jack Trice's teenage son had earlier gotten into a fistfight with a white boy, and the father of the white youngster raised a group of 15 men to go to the Trice home at 3:00 a.m. When they demanded young Trice be sent out of the house to them, Jack Trice opened gunfire, shooting some of the men and forcing the rest to flee. The Trices then abandoned their home and were gone by the time the lynchers returned with reinforcements.

Lynchings were attacks motivated by racism during which people were brutally murdered—sometimes in the night, like Thomas Wallis or the

Bakers, but often in a public way with many witnesses. Lynchings often involved the hanging of victims, but lynch mobs also killed people in other ways. Some victims endured terrible atrocities, such as being dragged behind a wagon, beaten, seeing loved ones harmed, being tied up and burned or having parts of their bodies dismembered, and other forms of torture. These vicious attacks occurred outside any due process of law, and sometimes with the knowledge or participation of law enforcement officials. State and local courts did little to punish lynchers, and if attackers were identified, penalties for killing African Americans in this way were small and considered to be in a different legal category from other kinds of murders. African-American men were the most common targets of lynch mobs, but women were also hurt and killed. Men were the most common members of white mobs or vigilante groups, but white conservative women were among those who supported the practice and participated in it as spectators.

African-American activists were not silent in the face of the injustices of lynching. In 1899 black churches observed Friday, June 2, as a day of fasting and prayer in which parishioners gathered to pray for justice for

Members of the white mob that ransacked Wilmington's black district in 1898 pose in front of a burned-down black business.

African Americans in the courts and for freedom from violence. In this unified effort to demonstrate, as the *New York Tribune* described it, "ceasing to be longer silent," ministers were asked to make the following Sunday, June 4, the occasion for sermons on these topics. Refusing to ignore lynching, activists scanned local newspapers and records and compiled and published data on the names of individuals who had been killed and the dates on which they died. Middle-class leaders raised the issue at public meetings and addressed it in editorials. Frances Ellen Watkins Harper, a writer and African-American feminist, spoke out at a meeting of the National Council of Women held in Washington, D.C., in February 1891. "A government which has power to tax a man in peace, [and] draft him in war, should have power to defend his life in the hour of peril" she told her audience. She criticized the federal government's failure to protect African Americans from violence or to provide them with justice for attacks that went unpunished on the local and state levels. An editorial entitled "How to Stop Lynching" published in the African-American women's journal the *Women's Era* in 1894 similarly asked why, if the federal government could regulate the use of money or the consumption of alcohol, it could not protect individuals from murderous mobs. The government "can stop lynching," the writer of the editorial concluded, "and until it does, it has on its hands the innocent blood of its murdered citizens."

The famed abolitionist Frederick Douglass also condemned the outrages against justice. Speaking to a large audience in 1886, he addressed the issue of the erosion of constitutional rights and the failure of the national government to offer protection to African-American citizens. The "Constitution has been slain in the house of its friends," he said. "The Federal Government, so far as we are concerned, has abdicated its functions and abandoned the objects for which the Constitution was framed. . . . They have promised us law, and abandoned us to anarchy; they have promised protection, and given us violence; they have promised us fish, and given us a serpent."

Among all the prominent African-American lecturers and journalists who took a public stand against lynching and worked tirelessly to bring an end to the practice, the most important was Ida B. Wells, the same young schoolteacher who had been thrown off the train outside Memphis in 1884. Just as her test of the constitutionality of racial segregation laws was sparked by her expulsion from the railroad passenger car, so her campaign against lynching began as the result of a specific incident. This time the incident of discrimination was not just a question of equality and dignity, but one of horror.

Three African-American small businessmen, Thomas Moss, Calvin McDowell, and Henry Stewart, owned and ran a very successful cooperative grocery store called the People's Grocery that was located in an African-American district of suburban Memphis known as the Curve. Moss and his wife Betty were the best friends of Ida B. Wells, and Wells was the godmother to their little girl, Maurine. Thomas Moss worked as a letter carrier by day and in the store by night, and he was very active in his church and his lodge. Because of his deep involvement in the community and its functions, everyone in the neighborhood knew him, and he was much beloved.

An economic rivalry soon developed between the People's Grocery and an older, less successful store that had been in the neighborhood longer and was owned by a white man named W. H. Barrett. Barrett had a deep resentment of Moss because of the success Moss and his partners had achieved in their business. That hatred deepened one day when a sidewalk quarrel broke out between black and white boys over a game of marbles. The African-American children bested the white children in the fight, whereupon the white parents, including Barrett, tried to take legal action against the black boys. The case was dismissed after the payment of small fines.

Tensions escalated, and the whites, still vengeful over the success of Thomas Moss's store, which had taken much of the business away from the white-owned grocery, organized a raid on the People's Grocery. They carried out the raid on a Saturday night, just as the store was closing. When they burst in, Moss was busy working on the store's accounts and McDowell was waiting on the last customers. Fearing that threats of violence would be carried out, friends of the partners had stationed themselves in the rear of the shop to guard the store. When the white men broke in through the back of the store, they were met by gunfire, and three of them were wounded.

The next morning there was a general raid of the black households and businesses near the Curve in order to locate the men who might have fired the shots that wounded the white vigilantes. Moss, McDowell, and Stewart were among those picked up and incarcerated in the jail. Black members of the Tennessee Rifles, a local militia that had an armory nearby, guarded the jail against white attacks for the first two nights. But when it was clear that the men who had been shot would recover, they felt that

Ida B. Wells with Maurine, Betty, and Tom Moss, Jr., the family of Memphis grocery store owner Thomas Moss, who was lynched in 1893.

tensions had passed and ceased their watchfulness. On the third night, a mob of white men was given access to the jail. They dragged Thomas Moss and his partners from their cells, loaded them aboard a railroad boxcar, took them outside the city limits, and lynched them. According to an eyewitness newspaper report of the lynching, McDowell tried to struggle with the lynchers and was mutilated before he was killed. Thomas Moss pleaded with his abductors to spare his life on behalf of his wife and children, including his young daughter Maurine and the unborn baby his wife was carrying. His plea was ignored, and when asked for a final statement before he was shot to death, he said: "Tell my people to go West—there is no justice for them here."

Hundreds of black residents of the Memphis area heeded Thomas Moss's last words. As Wells recalled in her memoirs, which were published after her death, the "shock to the colored people who knew and loved both Moss and McDowell was beyond description." And the violence had not ended. Whites rampaged through the black neighborhood the day after the murders, and a white mob looted goods from the People's Grocery and then destroyed the contents of the building. Black reaction was swift. Like the many migrants who had left farms and sharecropping plots before them and moved west or to black towns, many city dwellers sold their property and took their families to Oklahoma Territory. Two leading pastors in the Curve community organized their entire congregations to go. Meanwhile, those that stayed instituted an informal economic boycott of white businesses and stayed off city streetcars.

Ida B. Wells went into action. She had become part-owner of the *Memphis Free Speech* newspaper in 1889, and had lost her job as a teacher when she used its pages to protest the inferior quality of schools serving black students. After the murder of her dear friend Thomas Moss, she used the newspaper to encourage the black citizens of Memphis to leave town and went to churches to urge black parishioners to support the consumer boycott of white-owned and -run streetcars. The exodus from the city did more than help African Americans escape from the racist violence that had seized Memphis. It had a very real economic impact upon whites. After the lynching, as Wells recalled in her memoirs, white people discovered a "dearth of servants to cook their meals and wash their clothes and keep their homes in order, to nurse their babies and wait on their tables, to build their houses and do all classes of laborious work."

Wells set out to become an expert on lynching and to dispel some of the myths that were popularly accepted about why lynchings occurred. Thomas Moss was an upstanding citizen who was killed because he had acquired wealth and property. But white newspapers typically claimed that lynchings occurred because of black men's criminality. They especially claimed that lynchings happened because black men sexually assaulted white women. Wells knew that Thomas Moss was neither a criminal nor a rapist, and so she questioned these allegations about lynching in general. She personally investigated every lynching that she heard about in Mississippi in the months after Thomas Moss's death. Then she published an editorial that strongly implied that when the charge behind a lynching was rape, the actual fact of the matter was that in the overwhelming number of cases a black man and white woman had agreed to have a sexual relationship with each other. In short, no rape had occurred. "Nobody in this section of the country believes the old thread bare lie that Negro men rape white women," Wells wrote in her editorial for *Free Speech* in May 1892. The charge of rape was used to cover up the real violence—that of white men against black men. And the reasons for this violence was to deprive blacks of political and economic power—to keep them under the thumb of the white establishment.

When the editorial was printed, Wells was traveling in the North. She soon learned of the outcome. The same fate that had met the People's Grocery had been visited upon her newspaper office. Whites had gone to the *Free Speech* office at night, two days after the edition in which the editorial was published, and destroyed the type used to print the newspaper and all the furnishings of the office. They left a note saying that anyone who attempted to publish *Free Speech* again would be killed.

Ida B. Wells was not easily silenced. She was exiled from her home in the South because of her defense of black rights in the face of lawlessness, much as she had earlier in her life been expelled from the railway train for refusing to capitulate to unfair law. She took a newspaper job in the North and continued to claim for herself the right of free speech. She wrote editorials under the pen name Iola and prepared pamphlets on the lynching issue that challenged the standard view of lynchings that was presented in the white press, North and South. Once her writings began to be well known, she traveled widely as a lecturer, speaking on the issue of lynching to women's organizations, churches, and African-American groups.

Wells published her findings in a pamphlet called *Southern Horrors: Lynch Law in All Its Phases* in October 1892. The pamphlet was dedicated to African-American women in Manhattan and Brooklyn, because women's groups in the New York area had raised the funds to make the publication of her work possible. Victoria Earle Matthews, a freelance journalist and women's rights activist who in 1897 established the White Rose Mission, a settlement house that provided social services for black women workers and girls, and Maritcha Lyons, a Brooklyn schoolteacher, were very impressed when they read Wells's articles. They organized a series of small meetings in African-American households and church lecture rooms in which Wells presented information about lynching to groups of women. More than 250 black women attended these meetings and joined in forming a committee that organized a major fundraising event with Wells as the keynote speaker.

Though justice seemed to be sleeping in the last decades of the 19th century, African Americans like Wells were wide awake. Many African-American sharecroppers, like the people who had known Thomas Moss in Memphis and who decided to leave the city after his murder, migrated west, away from the lawlessness of the Deep South. Black industrial and farm workers tried forming labor and political coalitions with whites, and other individuals, like Wells and Homer A. Plessy, challenged the reversal of legal protections in court. All over the land people less well known than Wells and Plessy took their own private stands against discrimination, acting in defense of honor when personally confronted by racism. Black intellectuals wrote newspaper articles and books and gave speeches decrying injustices. And black middle-class people set about founding their own schools, churches, businesses, and self-help organizations. If the law offered no guarantee of equal access to existing institutions and services, or protection of black citizens' well-being from violence, then African Americans would create the means for achieving advancement on their own.

CHAPTER 4

SELF-HELP: "TO HEW OUT HIS OWN PATH"

> There is still doubt in many quarters as to the ability of the Negro . . .
> to hew out his own path . . . . Our pathway must be up through the soil
> . . . up through commerce, education, and religion!
>
> —Booker T. Washington in the Montgomery (Alabama) *Advertiser,*
> February 21, 1895

Johanna Bowen Redgrey was a midwife and healer who lived on a small farm on the outskirts of Tuskegee, Alabama, in the 1880s. She had been born into slavery near Richmond, Virginia, the daughter of an African-American mother and her mother's Irish-American master. When she was a teenager, her father sold her and her brothers to a white family who had a plantation in Macon County, Alabama. Johanna was a striking woman, six feet tall. She was muscular and strong from the field work she did, with a head of fiery reddish hair and a determined disposition to match her appearance. When the Civil War came, Johanna's brothers joined other young men who escaped from the plantation to try to fight for the North. She assumed they died in the attempt, because she never saw them again nor learned of their fate. She spent the latter part of the war and the early years after war's end working for wages for her former master. Then she met and married Lewis Redgrey.

Lewis Redgrey was a Native American who had spent part of his life in Mexico and spoke Spanish as well as English. He had a 55-acre farm outside Tuskegee, and Johanna went to live with him there. Together they raised hogs and corn and grew a cash crop of cotton. They were both important people in the community. Johanna Bowen Redgrey had gone to school and worked with doctors, and she knew a great deal about plants and herbs and how to make medicines. She delivered babies and nursed

George Washington Carver (second from right) with his students in the soil science laboratory at Tuskegee University.

77

both black and white families in times of illness or accident. She was deeply religious. She taught Sunday School and was very active with other women in the neighborhood in her own African Methodist Episcopal Zion church and in the Baptist church located on a nearby hill.

She and her husband were determined to provide good educations for their son and the other African-American children of Tuskegee. For them, making education available was the key to improving the lives of all African Americans. They were members of a committee of Tuskegee residents who worked to start a school in the town. They supported those who sent to Hampton Institute, a school in Virginia that trained African Americans for careers in nursing, teaching, farming, and trades, to find a schoolmaster to run it. They were among the group of black townspeople who gathered to greet the young teacher who came from Hampton. His name was Booker T. Washington and he arrived in Tuskegee in June 1881. "The place has a healthy and pleasant location—high and hilly—think I shall like it," Washington wrote home to a friend the day after his arrival. Classes in what would become Washington's famed Tuskegee Institute began a few days later, on July 4. The classes met in Johanna Bowen Redgrey's church on Zion Hill.

With their vision of a better future for their son and the black people in their community, Lewis and Johanna Bowen Redgrey had helped begin what would become one of the most important—and most controversial— educational enterprises in African-American history.

Church, family, neighbors, and school were at the heart of the Redgreys' lives. These connections between people were avenues for personal fulfillment, community, and mutual care. They also were means of self-expression. Strengthening and cherishing these kinds of social networks and avenues of uplift, and using their voices to present their own points of view, were crucial ways in which African Americans combated the racial injustices of the 1880s and 1890s.

The ability to worship freely, to marry and raise children without having them subject to others' control, and to learn to read and write were all freedoms that had been outside most black people's experience during slavery. This made them all the more precious to African Americans in the decades after emancipation. When it became clear in the post–Reconstruction era that the political rights and protections that had been promised after the end of the Civil War would not be theirs, African Americans set about forming their own separate institutions—schools,

A baptism in Aiken, South Carolina. Religious faith was one of the means by which African Americans dealt with the effects of racism. Through their churches they formed strong, supportive communities.

churches, hospitals, settlement houses, and newspapers—and making their own way. Through religion, family, and education African Americans built their own brand of freedom. They turned to each other to work together for the good of all black people.

In developing separate institutions and systems of self-help, African Americans used the power of words, both those that were written down and those that were spoken aloud. Despite a larger society where blackness was being belittled, souls were exalted through the hymns and sermons of the black church, and children were assured of their self-worth by tales told and passed down within the black family. Black schools gave students the power of literacy, the ability to read and write, and this opened to them new economic and intellectual possibilities. Black newspapers printed the opinions of black journalists, black intellectuals spoke at public events, black writers and poets published novels and books of poetry, and black men and women gathered together in literary societies to read and debate.

People who had not had the opportunity to learn to read could listen and speak. In doing so, they carried on an oral tradition that had long sustained a rich cultural heritage among African Americans from one generation to another. Those who could read passed newspapers and books from hand to hand, or read aloud to others. Black people had a voice, and the words they used gave them hope and strength.

African Americans did not speak in one voice, however. They had many points of view. One of the biggest debates among African Americans at the turn of the century was over the best approach to providing education to black people. Tuskegee Institute and its principal were at the center of this broad discussion.

Many of them supported Booker T. Washington's philosophy of industrial or vocational education, in which students would come to school to learn a trade and find a job. Others criticized it just as strongly. Many African-American intellectuals and political activists saw Washington's vision as a way of appeasing whites who felt that blacks should be manual laborers and not strive for high intellectual achievement—or as Washington himself often put it, that they should live by their hands rather than by their wits. But for these critics, higher education for black people, in which African Americans could enter academic programs in languages and music, the arts and humanities, science and research, or prepare for a profession, was as important as training for a vocation. Thus the debate about the nature of schooling was not only about economics and education, but about how best to react to white racism.

Washington believed that the "power of the mouth is not like the power of the object lesson." That is, he felt that black people could best

Booker T. Washington, first row, second from left, with the other members of Hampton Institute's graduating class of 1875.

advance by the quiet example of their cooperation with whites, by self-development, and by their skilled contributions to their mixed-race communities, rather than by overt militancy or protest. This view was scorned by leaders such as Frederick Douglass and Ida B. Wells. Douglass and Wells were among those who used the written and spoken word to confront injustices head-on. "One farm bought, one house built, one home neatly kept, one man the largest tax-payer and depositor in the local bank, one school or church maintained, one factory running successfully, one truck garden properly cultivated, one patient cured by a Negro doctor, one sermon well preached, one office well filled, one life cleanly lived," Washington wrote in 1895, "these will tell more in our favor than all the abstract eloquence that can be summoned to plead our cause."

The academic and vocational philosophies of education developed side by side in the 1880s and 1890s. This is one of the issues on which middle-class black people and poorer African Americans, and African Americans living in the North and in the South, differed. The debate about education and the types of work for which it should prepare students was directly related to ideas about African Americans' proper expectations regarding their status in society. Middle-class and Northern blacks were more likely to identify with and promote academic programs and more intellectual—and therefore elite—types of achievement. Rather than accommodate white views of black people's secondary status, they stressed their desire for equal rights and equal opportunities, including equal access to higher education.

At the same time, less privileged African-American students sometimes rebelled against industrial education curricula because they equated acquiring an education with an escape from manual labor. But others embraced Booker T. Washington's idea that agricultural and industrial labor and other forms of skilled work with the hands should be honored, and they believed that there was dignity in this kind of work. To many blacks living in the South, Washington's brand of education had its own flavor of militancy. Separatism and equality thus became the watchwords in the 1880s and 1890s for two different strategies for black advancement. Both had power, and the two perspectives often intersected in practice.

The story of the creation of the Tuskegee Institute exemplifies this combination of approaches. It is one example of the many separate institutions that were created by or for blacks at the end of the 19th century. Within a few weeks of his arrival in Tuskegee, Booker T. Washington was

joined by a young teacher named Olivia Davidson.
Together, with the help of the Tuskegee townspeople and
donations from white Northern philanthropists, they built
up the school.

Olivia Davidson had started teaching when she was
16. She taught in Mississippi and Tennessee before she
graduated from Washington's alma mater, Hampton
Institute, and from the Framingham State Normal School
in Massachusetts. When she came to Tuskegee in late
August 1881, she immediately set about getting to know
the people in the community and raising money for the
institute. She went door to door and talked to the people
of the town about their goals for education. With the aid
of black women like Johanna Bowen Redgrey, who were
eager to do anything they could to help, she organized
bake sales and community potluck suppers where women
contributed a dish they had prepared. Long picnic tables

*The first teacher
Booker T. Washington
hired for his Tuskegee
Institute was Olivia
Davidson. They
worked tirelessly to
raise funds and
recruit students for
the new school. Later,
in 1886, the two were
married.*

were covered with the donated food and the families of the town turned
out to celebrate together and support the new school. Soon after classes
began, Davidson organized a night of student literary entertainment, in
which the students selected and memorized poems and essays and recited
them to the black members of the town in an evening performance.

In June 1881 Washington began recruiting students for his new
school by speaking at both the Baptist and Methodist churches, inviting
anyone who was interested to come see him at his boardinghouse and
enroll. He rode around Macon County and familiarized himself with the
people in the countryside, reporting in his letters to friends in Virginia his
shock at the impoverished conditions of sharecropper families and the lack
of books and other materials in the one-room rural schools that were
already in operation.

There were 30 students in the first class that began school in the
Methodist church on Independence Day 1881. They varied in age from
teenagers to middle-aged adults. Most of them were public school teachers
who had come to receive better training so they could in turn pass that
knowledge on to the rural children who were their pupils.

In time, as the result of Davidson and Washington's efforts, the school
acquired land, the former Bowen plantation, and made plans to build a new
building. Washington turned his mind to business, and the curriculum of

the school soon combined book-learning classes with various manual labor tasks. The manual labor served two functions. It prepared students for skilled jobs in industry and agriculture, and it earned money immediately for the development of the school.

Students worked hard outside the classroom. They cleared land for a cash crop of cotton. They made bricks that would be used in the construction of Tuskegee Institute buildings or sold to local business owners for use in the town. The profits were turned back into expanding the programs and facilities of the school and hiring new teachers. Washington hoped that the kind of business relationships that would be built up between the school and the white townspeople through brickmaking and other student enterprises would overcome whites' racist ideas. He also hoped that the influential white residents of Tuskegee would support the school out of self-interest because of the quality products the students produced and the value of the students' skilled employment. Thus the school served, on a small scale, as a model or experiment for Washington's philosophy of race relations, which he felt should be applied to the nation as a whole.

The ceremonies that marked the end of the Tuskegee Institute's first year were symbolic of the combination of forces that had given birth to

A carpentry class at Tuskegee Institute. Washington believed in providing male students with training in job-related fields such as carpentry, brickmaking, crop management, furniture making, and barrel making.

Washington and Davidson's educational enterprise. People came from all over town, from the countryside, and from as far away as Hampton, Virginia, to meet on Zion Hill in Tuskegee. The students had decorated the church with arches of roses, and evergreens and bouquets of roses were interspersed throughout the room. The spoken word was central to all the events, as students began and ended the day with recitations and songs, and educators and ministers gave orations. A big picnic supper was served outside. At midday, a procession was formed and the people wound their way from the town to the new land that had been purchased for the school on its outskirts.

When they paraded from the church to the new school grounds, the students and citizens of Tuskegee symbolically moved from the school's past into its future. The church building was soon replaced as the location for the school when classrooms and dormitories were built. Two years later, there were 169 students studying at the school. By 1900, when Booker T. Washington published his autobiography, *Up from Slavery,* there were 1,400 students enrolled, and more than 100 instructors. The Tuskegee Institute was a thriving school and economic enterprise with its own working farm, sawmill, foundry, brickyard, and blacksmith, machine, woodworking, barrelmaking, and print shops. As Washington's daughter, Portia Washington, wrote in July 1900, the industrial institute had become "really a small village," occupied and run by African Americans, and the goal of "Principal Washington is to make it an object-lesson, or model community for the masses in general."

By the 1890s, Washington, who made extensive public speaking tours to promote the school, had become a famous and powerful man. White receptiveness to the vocational emphasis of his school had made him into a recognized spokesman on racial matters, and he wielded far-reaching political influence from behind the scenes. The little school that the Redgreys had helped begin had become the center of a social movement, with Washington at its head.

Washington turned to three different well-educated black women to share his work and his private life. During Tuskegee's first year, he married his college girlfriend, Fanny Norton Smith. Their daughter Portia was born in 1883. Fanny Washington died a year later, leaving Washington alone with the little girl. In August 1886 Olivia Davidson became Booker T. Washington's second wife. She had long been his partner in the school, teaching science classes at Tuskegee; acting as the

Booker T. Washington was a powerful, dynamic speaker who travelled across the country promoting his school.

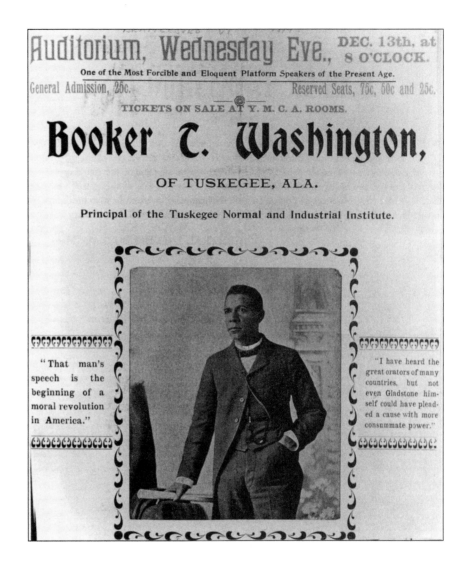

Auditorium, Wednesday Eve., DEC. 13th, at 8 O'CLOCK.

One of the Most Forcible and Eloquent Platform Speakers of the Present Age.

General Admission, 25c. Reserved Seats, 75c, 50c and 25c.

TICKETS ON SALE AT Y. M. C. A. ROOMS.

Booker T. Washington,

OF TUSKEGEE, ALA.

Principal of the Tuskegee Normal and Industrial Institute.

"That man's speech is the beginning of a moral revolution in America."

"I have heard the great orators of many countries, but not even Gladstone himself could have pleaded a cause with more consummate power."

school's Lady Principal by overseeing the female students; and making fund-raising tours of the North. After their marriage she continued her work with the school. She cared for Portia and gave birth to two sons, Baker and Ernest. But disaster came. Despite her energetic work, Olivia Davidson Washington had always been frail in health. Soon after Ernest was born, the chimney in the Washingtons' house caught fire during the night, burning down the house. Booker T. Washington was away raising money for the school at the time. Olivia and the children escaped the flames, but she had been very ill after childbirth and her condition

A November 1902, history class at Tuskegee. By this time, Tuskegee was a thriving school, with a growing national reputation.

worsened after the fire. She never recovered. She died in a hospital in Boston in May 1889.

Four years later Booker T. Washington married for a third time. He turned for companionship and help with his children to Margaret (Maggie) Murray, a teacher from Mississippi who had been serving as the Lady Principal at Tuskegee since May 1890.

Margaret Murray Washington had been educated at Fisk University, in Nashville, where she was associate editor of the school newspaper and president of a campus literary society. She began teaching at Tuskegee in 1889. Like Olivia Washington, Margaret Murray Washington believed strongly in the importance of education for African-American girls and women. In 1886 Olivia Washington gave a speech at the Alabama State Teachers Association in which she said that the best way to improve the lives of African Americans was to recognize the contributions of great women and to develop and encourage black girls to high achievement. Maggie Washington shared this belief. She took on Olivia Washington's role as the power behind women's education at Tuskegee.

The Tuskegee curriculum combined academic and vocational training for both male and female students, with an emphasis for everyone on preparing for an occupation. Tuskegee students took classes in art, music, and literature, botany, chemistry, and mathematics. In addition, they all enrolled in some program of practical training. All of these training courses

As Tuskegee's Lady Principal, Margaret Murray Washington was responsible for the education of girls and women at the school. She demanded that they be given the opportunity to study agriculture and other disciplines that had previously been considered unsuitable for girls.

were based on gaining skills for employment in occupations that already existed for black people in the South. Within Booker T. Washington's scheme, boys and girls were thought to be suited to different kinds of occupations and thus to separate sorts of classes in their education. Young men trained in agriculture or in trades such as carpentry, blacksmithing, mechanics, or furniture making. Young women were directed toward classes in housekeeping and domestic science. These courses would prepare girls for work in household service, which was the main source of wage employment for black women at the time, and also to run their own homes according to up-to-date Victorian standards. Female students could also learn advanced sewing so they could make a living as dressmakers and hatmakers.

Recognizing that women could do many kinds of agricultural work that could be turned to profit on a family farm, Margaret Murray Washington insisted that female students also be given opportunities to study agricultural methods. The "outdoor work" for women included dairying, raising poultry and livestock, and growing flowers and vegetables for market. Margaret Murray Washington considered these forms of expertise more healthy and independent options for black women in seeking a livelihood than factory work or leaving the rural areas of the South for work in cities.

The agricultural department of Tuskegee Institute as a whole was directed, beginning in 1896, by George Washington Carver. An 1894 graduate of Iowa State University, Carver was a brilliant scientist and teacher who also painted beautiful pictures of fruits and flowers. His experiments in botany and innovations in soil analysis and enrichment made the Tuskegee Institute's experimental farm into a showcase of high-yield crops. He encouraged farmers to grow crops such as sweet potatoes and peanuts in addition to cotton, and to rotate the kinds of crops grown in their fields to maintain the richness of the soil. He also invented industrial uses for the by-products of these diversified crops, such as the shells of peanuts. In 1899 he began what he called his "Moveable School," a large wagon equipped with farm machinery and exhibits that was drawn by mules around the dirt roads of the countryside. Carver and his assistants used the wagon to bring lessons they taught in their laboratories and classrooms to

the African Americans farming throughout the county. Johanna Bowen Redgrey's granddaughter, Frances, was among the students whom Carver taught in formal science classes at the institute.

Many students at Tuskegee, both men and women, trained to become teachers, and Tuskegee graduates ran rural schools throughout the South and taught at other colleges. The Tuskegee Institute hospital, opened in 1892, served as a nurses' training school. The hospital and nursing program are representative of a number of black institutions that were founded between 1890 and 1930. Black women like Johanna Bowen Redgrey had long served an important function in their communities as traditionally trained lay healers, nurses, and midwives. At the end of the 19th century, black women and men participated in the movement to professionalize nursing, adding clinical training, hospital experience, and basic courses in nutrition, sanitation, and primary care to the kind of practical knowledge and informal apprenticeships that had trained women like Redgrey. Black hospitals provided opportunities for physicians who had been barred from working in white institutions to practice medicine and surgery. The formation of hospitals staffed with black physicians and nurses—like the founding of schools, businesses, and community organizations—was one more important form of African-American institution-building in the post-Reconstruction period.

George Washington Carver was born a slave in 1864 but went on to become a scientist of international repute. As the leader of Tuskegee's agricultural department he dedicated his efforts to developing methods that would help farmers throughout the South.

While she oversaw the domestic training, outdoor work, and professional education of women students in teaching and nursing at Tuskegee Institute, Margaret Murray Washington extended the principles that were being taught at the school into practice in the town. Following in the footsteps of Olivia Davidson Washington, she concentrated on ways of organizing the women of Tuskegee, especially those who worked as tenant farmers or sharecroppers and lived outside of town.

In the 1890s she devised a plan for bringing together the middle-class black women who worked as instructors at Tuskegee, or were married to male members of the faculty, and working-class or lower-class women who did not have the benefit of formal education. As she explained in an essay called "Helping the Mothers," which Booker T. Washington printed as part of his 1904 book *Working with the Hands*, the "country women, tired of the monotony of their lives, came crowding into the village every Saturday." On one Saturday, Margaret Murray Washington went into town and sent a small boy around to the women, asking them to come to a room above "a very dilapidated store which stands on the main street of the village." Six came the first night, and thus began the meetings of the Mothers' Union. Held every Saturday of the school year, the meetings attracted more than 300 women a week by 1900.

When the women came together, Washington wrote, "we talked it all over, the needs of our women, the best ways of helping each other."

A home economics class at Hampton Institute, Hampton, Virginia. Founded in 1868, Hampton was designed primarily to train young African Americans as teachers and leaders in the black community.

Women came long distances on foot to attend the meetings. Among them were Johanna Bowen Redgrey, who brought her young granddaughter along. Many women brought their girls with them, and soon a lending library and classes for the children were organized. Meanwhile, Margaret Washington founded the Tuskegee Women's Club for the instructors and faculty wives on the school campus. The middle-class women founded newspaper reading clubs, staffed the library, and provided Saturday day care. They also visited poor women in their homes in the country, offering advice about improving the standard of living for the farming families.

Much of this advice involved teaching middle-class ways to poor people. The sharecropper women were taught about bathing regularly and wearing more formal apparel, maintaining housekeeping and churchgoing schedules, growing vegetable gardens to supplement a diet of cornmeal and pork, and doing many of the things on the farm that women students were taught to do at the school. The Victorian values passed from middle-class to poor women extended to matters of demeanor. The well-to-do women were judgmental about the working women's conduct and believed they had the right, by their superior social standing, to correct it. As Portia Washington explained, "Most of these women are from the heart of the country, where their chances of refinement are few. If it were not for these meetings, many of the women would be hanging around the streets talking and laughing in a very coarse manner. As it is, they are taught to see the wrong in such actions."

Monthly workshops were held on topics suggested by the country women, with lessons written up in pamphlet form and distributed from home to home. These booklets contained advice on parenting, manners, household repair, and farming, and "also little recipes which any woman may need in her country home, especially when there is sickness in the family." Women students joined in by establishing a house on the grounds of an old 2,000-acre plantation where 75 black families lived in sharecropper cabins. A female student lived in the house and taught reading to the parents and children that were farming the land around it. Sewing, cooking, gardening, and housekeeping classes were soon added.

The kind of outreach and organization among women that Margaret Murray Washington set in motion in Tuskegee was happening among black women all around the nation. Excluded from formal social services, health care institutions, and charity organizations run by whites, black women served their communities with their own associations.

Home for Aged Colored Women in Account with Harriet W. Rothermel, Treasurer.	
1890-91. TO CASH RECEIVED.	1890-91. BY CASH PAID.

1890-91. TO CASH RECEIVED.		1890-91. BY CASH PAID.	
Entrance Fees	$1,200 00	Wages	$537 80
St. John's Church — Collections, $19.00: Donations -- Mrs. E. A. Gammell, $50.00; Mrs. Chas. Fletcher, $50.00; Mr. John Nicholas Brown, $20.00. Life Membership — Mr. T. P. J. Goddard, $25.00	164 00	Fuel	152 85
		Gas	2 17
		Water Tax	18 92
		Ice	17 74
Grace Church	49 50	Provisions	367 70
St. Stephen s Church — Collections, $34.00; Life Membership — Rhoda P. Bullock, $25 00	59 00	Druggist	4 14
First Congregational Church	27 00	Clothing and Kitchen Furnishings	63 74
Union Congregational Church	12 00	Printing, Advertising, Stationery, Etc	15 83
Beneficent Congregational Church	11 00	Matron, for Incidental Expenses	46 32
Westminster Congregational Church	35 50		
Central Congregational Church	55 90	Total Expenditures	$1,227 21
First Baptist Church — Collections, $23.90; Life Membership — Miss Maria M. Benedict, $25.00	48 90	Balance in Treasury	944 57
Collection Box	29 28		$2,171 78
Ladies' Benign Society of Providence	31 70		
Woman's Home Missionary Society of Union Congregational Church, Newport	5 00		
Through Mrs. A. A. Angell	10 00		
Through Mrs. E. M. Bannister — Collections, $72.16; Life Memberships — Miss Elizabeth Carlile, $25.00; Miss Eva K. Davis, $25.00; Mrs. George Henry, $25.00	147 16	PROVIDENCE, April 23, 1891.	
Proceeds from Bazaar held at Home	204 05		
Proceeds from Charades given by children of Mrs. George E. Barstow	2 00	I have examined the foregoing account, and compared it with the vouchers, and found it to be correct.	
A Friend	10 00	OREN WESTCOTT, *Auditor*.	
Miscellaneous Contributions	60 90		
Interest on Deposit	8 89		
	$2,171 78		

A page from the annual report of the Home for Aged Colored Women in Providence, Rhode Island. African Americans formed Mothers' Clubs, neighborhood unions, benevolent societies, and settlement houses to help provide food, health care, and other support services to the ill, to children and the aged, and to new migrants to the cities, including single young women.

Benevolent groups in the cities and women's auxiliaries organized through churches had long provided health care to the ill and clothing and food to those who needed it. In the mid-1890s homes for black working women and for the aged, and nurseries and day care centers for the children of working mothers were established in several cities in the North. Although Margaret Murray Washington began a settlement house in a rural Southern setting, the majority of settlement houses begun in the 1890s by middle-class men and women were located in the North and Midwest. Settlement houses provided classes and job services, including literacy training and information about good nutrition and child care.

One of the most important settlements for black women was the White Rose Mission and Industrial Association, founded in 1897 by Victoria Earle Matthews, one of the women who had organized Ida B. Wells's pathbreaking public lecture in New York. The home was established to help young working women new to the city. Like Margaret Murray Washington's domestic science curriculum at Tuskegee, the mission offered classes in cooking, laundry, and sewing—teaching the new migrants the city skills that could be converted into jobs in household service. Matthews also established a library of books about black history, and taught neighborhood women to be proud of their heritage.

Black settlement house residents in both the North and the South, including those at the White Rose Mission, also became involved in expanding the kindergarten movement, which in the 1890s was an innovative approach to early childhood education. Settlements and churches served as centers for community forums and lecture tours. Booker T. Washington came to speak to working women and the middle-class women organizers at the White Rose Mission, as did other prominent intellectuals and writers of the day.

In addition to attending public lectures, middle-class men and women formed literary societies that met in members' homes. These societies served a political purpose for middle-class women who were excluded from many of the public functions in which middle-class men participated. They were also one more way in which African Americans exercised the power of the word. The secular benevolent associations, church charity groups, settlement houses, and literary societies were in some ways schools for adults, especially for women. They provided a chance for middle-class women to acquire new speaking and organizing skills. Through their activism in these groups, women learned how to hold meetings, coordinate tasks among people of different backgrounds and interests, organize programs, raise funds, do publicity, and to speak with confidence to audiences and participate in group debate. Many of them would use these skills in broader forums of social and political reform.

Literary society meetings provided a chance for educated middle-class African-American men and women to discuss books and debate the current events of the day, and to give recitations and lectures to one another. The Bethel Literary and Historical Association, for example, was a key literary society in Washington, D.C. It was founded in 1881 by church activists interested in education, and it featured several black women lecturers and debaters. Topics presented at the society meetings ranged from heroes of the antislavery movement and other black history topics to discussions of music, social reform, and politics. The separate education of the sexes was one of the frequently debated issues.

The membership of literary societies, churches, and settlement programs often overlapped. One of the leaders of the Bethel Literary and Historical Association was Amanda Bowen, who also directed the Sojourner Truth Home for Working Girls of Washington, D.C., in 1895. The home

This page from the annual report of the African Methodist Episcopal Church from 1890 highlights the church's desire to spread its message to what it calls the "Darker Races."

was supported by the members of the Metropolitan African Methodist Episcopal Church.

The links between the Metropolitan AME Church, the literary society, and the founding of the home for girls in Washington, D.C., or between the AME Zion Church of Tuskegee, the Mothers' Clubs, and the founding of the Tuskegee Institute in Alabama, were not coincidental. These examples are indicative of the way that churches influenced the creation of black social welfare and educational institutions around the country.

The church had long been a mainstay of African-American life. Faith and spirituality were important means of maintaining and building self-worth and group support during the days of slavery. In the post–Reconstruction era, when Jim Crow practices were being made into law throughout the South, the church continued to be the focus of many African-Americans' social and inner lives. The independence of black churches within mixed-race small towns and cities, and the willingness of members to contribute money and volunteer work to their churches, made the church the strongest single institution of African-American self-help in the 1880s and 1890s.

Churches were places of worship. But they were also the primary places that African Americans used as assembly halls and community centers. Many, like the church in Tuskegee that housed the first classes of the Tuskegee Institute, were directly connected to schooling in their communities.

In the same year that Tuskegee Institute was founded in the church buildings in Tuskegee, Spelman College for women began as the Atlanta Baptist Female Seminary in the basement of the Friendship Baptist Church in Atlanta, Georgia. It began as an elementary and secondary school for adult women, offering literacy classes to women who had not had a prior opportunity to learn to read and write, and giving religious instruction. Over the years, it broadened its programs and evolved into a full four-year college. Like Tuskegee Institute and other African-American schools, it offered classes to prepare students for occupa-

The students and faculty of Provident Hospital and Nurse Training School in Chicago in 1895. Founded in 1891, this was one of several black hospital nursing schools established in the 1890s.

tions in teaching and household service. A nurses' training program was added in 1886.

African-American women were active as policymakers in education in addition to being students and teachers in the classrooms. The church was an important factor here as well. Beginning in the 1880s, black women church activists organized state conventions where they met to advocate support of black Baptist-owned schools for higher education and missionary work. Conventions were held in Alabama, Arkansas, Kentucky, Missouri, Mississippi, West Virginia, and other states. Many of these state conventions published their own newspapers, and their members also wrote columns on women's and educational issues for general Baptist publications. In 1887 more than 40 newspapers were being produced by black Baptists. Most of these were published in the South.

The work of church members was crucial to providing social services to black people who lived nearby. Churches were also places to hold community theater productions, suppers, and programs, and to gather to discuss local issues and current events. In the midst of a larger society that denied leadership roles to African Americans, churches provided opportunities for ministers and members to speak their thoughts and hold positions of authority. Though church activities were spearheaded by the ministers who served them, and community at large looked to these preachers as spokesmen for their congregations, the community work and fund-raising was done mainly by their women members.

The black church programs, hospitals, newspapers, settlement houses, and schools that were established in the last decades of the 19th century left no doubt about the African American's ability to, as Booker T. Washington had put it in 1895, "hew out his [or her] own path."

Washington had told African-American readers that their "pathway must be . . . up through commerce, education, and religion!" While many African Americans were busy working with schools and building their faith through action in their churches, others applied the principles of self-help and collective institution building to commercial and political fields. They organized lecture tours, promoted black businesses, and founded newspapers and associations that argued for African-American economic and civil rights. By the end of the century African-American soldiers would also find themselves fighting in another war. This time they would bring issues about the duties and rights of black citizenship beyond the borders of the United States.

AFRO-AMERICAN MONUMENT.

CHAPTER 5

LEADERSHIP: "SHOW US THE WAY"

Who shall come after thee, out of the clay—
Learned one and leader to show us the way?

—Paul Laurence Dunbar, "Alexander Crummell—Dead," *Lyrics of the Hearthside,* 1899

There are those of his own race who deny that Booker T. Washington is a leader of his race; that he stands in the place where Frederick Douglass stood. . . . Booker T. Washington . . . at the Atlanta Exposition . . . revealed himself to the nation as a leader out of the forge of slavery who had laid the foundation deep in the hearts of the people.

—T. Thomas Fortune, *Boston Transcript,* July 5, 1899

O ne of the most important moments in the life of Booker T. Washington came on the sunny late afternoon of September 18, 1895, when he walked to the front of a stage to give a speech to a huge gathering of business executives and visitors at the Cotton States and International Exposition in Atlanta, Georgia.

The audience at this big commercial event had come to celebrate the emergence of a new post–Civil War South. As Washington recalled in his autobiography, he rose to speak and faced an audience "of two thousand people, composed mostly of Southern and Northern whites." The black people in attendance sat in a separate gallery. The master of ceremonies had just introduced Washington as a great educator, with no reference to his color, but when the audience saw a tall, distinguished black man rise to give the speech, their applause wavered and died out in disapproval. Washington nevertheless strode forward and took his place on the stage.

This poster depicting scenes from the history of African Americans, beginning with the arrival of the first slaves in 1619 (top left), was prepared for the Tennessee Centennial Exposition held in Nashville in 1897.

Washington gave a short and simple oration that expressed opinions he had shared with other audiences many times before. But this time his statement was greeted in a new way. It was publicized, reprinted, and accepted among whites—and damned by some blacks—as a manifesto of black accommodation to white supremacy in the South. In preaching a message that was acceptable to white Southerners—the gradual uplift of blacks in the name of the mutual economic progress of blacks and whites, and thus of the South as a whole—Washington's speech in Atlanta set the tone for race policy and race relations in the United States for decades to come.

The speech also signaled the arrival of a new leader among African Americans. That September day in Atlanta marked the true beginning of widespread recognition of Washington as the most prominent spokesman for African Americans in his time. In his speech Washington displayed the combination of defiance and compromise that would continue to mark his leadership for the rest of his life. The statement of defiance and proclamation of black selfhood and personal authority Washington made silently—by standing up before the Atlanta audience. The compromise could be found in the openly expressed message of his words. Washington's speech symbolizes a time when new black leaders appeared in many fields of political and cultural achievement, and when themes of compromise or accommodation, self-assertion and protest, were found simultaneously in the public life and leadership of black people.

Washington began his oration by telling a story about a ship that had been lost at sea for many days. The crew was thirsty, and when they finally sighted another ship, they called out three times for water. "Cast down your bucket where you are," answered the people on the other vessel. When the thirsty sailors did lower a bucket, they were surprised to draw it back up full of fresh water. Without knowing it, they had drifted near the mouth of a river and the water that flowed under their ship was not undrinkable salt water, as they thought, but good water for drinking.

Washington's story was a metaphor for what he felt black people in the South needed to do. Instead of fleeing and looking for what they needed elsewhere, like those who had gone from Louisiana or Mississippi to Kansas, or asking for aid from without, like those who looked to the North, or trekked from the fields to the cities, he counseled that they remain in the South and find there ways to improve their condition. In his speech, Washington struck a bargain with white Southerners and Northerners in positions of power. According to this deal, black labor would remain in the

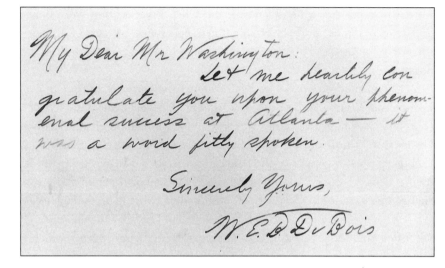

South and concentrate on developing better agriculture and commerce. White businessmen and landowners would benefit from retaining the hard work and services of African Americans. They would also benefit from the commercial and industrial progress that would come with investment in the education and business enterprises of blacks. In return, both races would act, as Washington said in his speech, in "determination to administer absolute justice, in a willing obedience among all classes to the mandates of law."

The other part of the bargain that Washington suggested was the part that most disturbed black leaders who disagreed with his approach. In exchange for greater future material prosperity and the promise of more evenhanded administration of the law, African Americans, Washington implied, would not make immediate or forceful claims for equal rights and opportunities. Nor would they attempt to share in the social privileges enjoyed by whites in public and private settings. In the most famous line of the speech, which became known as the "Atlanta Compromise," Washington promised that "in all things that are purely social we can be as separate as the fingers, yet one as the hand in all things essential to mutual progress."

This metaphor of the hand and the fingers was greeted with great applause by the white audience, the very same audience that had grumbled when Washington first took the stage. The reaction of the blacks who heard Washington that day was more cryptic. James Creelman, a reporter for the *New York World*, wrote on the front page of the *World's* September 19, 1895, edition that at the speech's end "most of the Negroes in the audience were crying, perhaps without knowing just why." Whether they were shedding tears of intense pride in Washington's appearance, or tears of dismay over what his message might mean for African Americans in the future, was not recorded.

We do know how other leaders reacted. The journalist T. Thomas Fortune saw Washington's advice as a triumph of reconciliation and leadership. The black novelist Charles W. Chesnutt saw it in another way. In his 1903 article "The Disfranchisement of the Negro," he observed that "Southern white men may applaud this advice as wise, because it fits in with their purposes." But telling blacks "to go slow in seeking to enforce their civil and political rights . . . in effect, means silent submission to injustice."

Washington explained the philosophy behind his speech when he described the Atlanta event in his autobiography, *Up from Slavery,* which was published in book form in 1901 after being serialized the previous year. The book, like the speech itself, was designed to appeal primarily to a white audience. "I believe," Washington wrote, that "it is the duty of the Negro—as the greater part of the race is already doing—to deport himself modestly in regard to political claims, depending upon the slow but sure influences that proceed from the possession of property, intelligence, and high character for the full recognition of his political rights." This was a policy of appeasement.

Washington's speech symbolized a key change of personalities and techniques in the national leadership of African Americans. The 1880s and 1890s saw the deaths of many members of an older generation of African-American activists, who had led the movement to abolish slavery. The great abolitionist, orator, and women's rights advocate Sojourner Truth died in 1883. The passing of leadership from the militancy of the past to the accommodation of Washington in the present was best signified by the death of Frederick Douglass. Douglass, who had often appeared on the same platform with Sojourner Truth, had long dominated the political stage as an orator and commentator on current events. He died in Washington, D.C., on February 20, 1895, just six months before Washington spoke at the Atlanta Exposition.

In June 1895, W. E. B. Du Bois became the first African American to receive a Ph.D. degree from Harvard University. This, too, was a significant event in shaping the new standard of leadership. The young Du Bois, like Washington, would soon be recognized as one of the leaders of African-American thought.

This montage from an 1896 publication features five of the most prominent black leaders of the era: T. Thomas Fortune, Booker T. Washington, Ida B. Wells, I. Garland Penn, and, in the center, Frederick Douglass.

1. T. THOMAS FORTUNE, Journalist.　　2. BOOKER T. WASHINGTON, Educator.

3. HON. FREDERICK DOUGLASS, Statesman.

4. I. GARLAND PENN, Author, Orator;　　5. MISS IDA B. WELLS,
Chief Commissioner, Atlanta Exposition.　　Lecturer, Defender of the Race.

Because of the erosion of civil rights in the late 19th century, black leadership had also declined in party politics and government. Although 22 African Americans were elected to the U.S. Congress between 1870 and the turn of the century, the post–Civil War white backlash against an integrated Republican party in the South effectively ended Republican power and Reconstruction reforms by 1877.

In the last three decades of the 19th century, 20 African Americans were elected to the House of Representatives. Most of these were elected in the 1870s. Eight represented districts in South Carolina, four were from North Carolina, three from Alabama, and one each was from Virginia, Georgia, Florida, Louisiana, and Mississippi. Two black men—Hiram Revels and Blanche K. Bruce—served in the U.S. Senate as senators from the state of Mississippi.

Though many of these leaders were ex-slaves, a large proportion of black officeholders (in relation to the overall African-American population) were freedmen before the Civil War. Some (such as James T. Rapier of Alabama, Blanche K. Bruce, and Josiah T. Walls of Florida, who were all planters) were wealthy entrepreneurs or landowners, coming from a business class like that of many white candidates for office. But all, regardless of their backgrounds, had an essential political base in the majority black communities in the districts they represented.

These African-American men were elected to serve in the Virginia General Assembly in 1887–88.

Many had come to political leadership after gaining experience as leaders in black education or in the black churches in their communities or states. Blanche K. Bruce of Mississippi, for example, was a sheriff, a tax collector, and a superintendent of schools in his county before moving into state and then national office.

After the end of Reconstruction in the late 1870s, black Republican politicians saw the need to form alliances with white Democrats and provide patronage to white constituents in order to stay in office. These compromises made it possible for some to retain their positions into the 1880s, but by the 1890s Jim Crow legal disenfranchisement crippled black political influence on the state level.

Blanche K. Bruce was first elected to the U.S. Senate in 1874, when he was 34 years old. By working closely with fellow black Mississippi politicians John R. Lynch and James Hill and carefully distributing federal positions to white constituents, he was able to exert power over state Republican politics in Mississippi and win a reputation for conservative leadership in Washington. He left the Senate in 1881, but returned to Washington as a political appointee in the Treasury Department during the presidencies of Republicans James A. Garfield (1881–85) and Benjamin Harrison (1889–93). Bruce died in 1898.

His colleague, Congressman Lynch, had a similar career. John R. Lynch left Congress in 1883, and, like Bruce, held an appointment in the Treasury Department during the Harrison presidency. He then sought leadership positions outside of electoral politics, becoming a lawyer in the District of Columbia and serving in the U.S. Army during the Spanish-American War.

Because of the effectiveness of the disenfranchisement of black voters, the new leaders who came to the forefront in the 1880s and 1890s were not elected officials. Sometimes they were designated as representatives of African-American opinion by whites, and sometimes they rose to this stature through the esteem with which they were held by fellow African Americans who felt that they spoke what was in their own hearts and minds. The influence of leaders like Booker T. Washington, W. E. B. Du Bois, Ida B. Wells, and T. Thomas Fortune was far-reaching. Each of these leaders was involved in the formation of important organizations that reflected the needs and desires of different segments of the African-American population. And their ideas and chosen methods of activism had an impact upon African-American history well into the 20th century.

Booker T. Washington's Tuskegee Negro Conference, first held in 1892, is an example of the kind of leadership found in that era. According to the circular advertising the meeting, Washington's aim was to "bring together for a quiet conference, not the politicians and those usually termed the 'leading colored people,' but representatives of the masses—the bone and sinew of the race—the common, hard working farmers with a few of the best ministers and teachers." There were two goals, the circular continued: "First, to find out the actual industrial, moral and educational condition of the masses. Second, to get as much light as possible on what is the most effective way for the young men and women whom the Tuskegee Institute and other institutions are educating to use their education in helping the masses of the colored people to lift themselves up." Washington expected about 75 farmers, educators, and preachers to come on February 23. Instead, about 500 men and women showed up.

They spent the morning sharing with each other information about their lives, describing who owned the land in the regions where they lived, what crops were grown, what their homes were like, where they worshipped, and where their children went to school. In the afternoon they drafted a set of resolutions. The resolutions did not deal with political or civil rights. They were about methods of self-help and ways to climb the socioeconomic ladder to the middle class. They urged all to buy land, build larger houses and schools, "give more attention to the character of their leaders, especially ministers and teachers," and stay out of debt. The desire of women for greater respect and opportunities was reflected in the resolution "to treat our women better."

Tuskegee Conferences were held annually after 1892, and by 1895, the year of Washington's Atlanta Exposition address, so many people were attending that the overall conference was broken into separate conferences for farmers, teachers, and women. Long working hours and domestic violence were among the issues the women brought up as their concerns at the February 1895 conference.

The Tuskegee Negro Conferences represented discussion and change from the bottom up (although it was under the careful stewardship of Booker T. Washington and his colleagues), but the formation of the American Negro Academy represented leadership from the top down. Planned as an elite organization, the academy was founded in Washington,

Alexander Crummell, a leader of the Episcopal church, was the first president of the American Negro Academy. Formed in 1897, the academy was the first major black learned society in the country.

D.C., in 1897 and designed to be the first major learned society for African-American intellectuals. Its first president was Alexander Crummell, long an Episcopal church leader and an inspiration to many of the younger men in the group. Crummell was one of the older generation of leaders, like Frederick Douglass and Sojourner Truth, whose life spanned much of the 19th century. He lived and worked in Liberia, West Africa, for many years and was one of the major theorists of the early Pan-African move- ment, which encouraged political unity among the peoples of the African diaspora. Crummell died the year after the academy was founded.

A person could not just join the academy. Participation was restricted to the select few who were nominated and elected to membership by those who were already members. The founders included Du Bois, sociologist Kelly Miller, and poet Paul Laurence Dunbar. Only one woman, the Washington, D.C., educator and feminist theorist Anna Julia Cooper, was invited to join the men in the academy.

The purposes of the academy included the promotion of scholarly work by black Americans and the refutation of theories and beliefs that stereotyped and demeaned African Americans. In his 1897 speech "The Conservation of Races," Du Bois spelled out the academy's purposes: "It aims at once to be the epitome and expression of the intellect of the black . . . people of America, the exponent of the race ideals of one of the world's great races." Du Bois succeeded Crummell as president of the American Negro Academy in 1898.

At the same time that the academy was beginning, W. E. B. Du Bois was busy conducting his survey of African-American urban life in Philadel- phia. Soon after finishing the survey, Du Bois became a professor at Atlanta University, where he directed the elite answer to Washington's Tuskegee conferences, the annual Atlanta Conference on Negro Problems. These conferences, held each May at Atlanta University, created a forum for African-American social scientists and other intellectuals. They gathered to exchange their research and ideas and to organize a series of sociological studies about various aspects of African-American life in the South. Studies in the 1890s focused on African-American mortality and life in the cities, and African Americans in business.

Like the Tuskegee conferences, the second Atlanta University gather- ing included a separate women's meeting, which focused on issues of moth- erhood, childraising, and early childhood education. Educators and activists Lucy Laney and Adella Hunt Logan were among the participants who gave

papers or addresses there. In 1883, Laney founded a school in Augusta, Georgia, that became the Haines Normal and Industrial Institute. She was a pioneer in kindergarten education and nurses' training. Logan was a teacher at Tuskegee Institute, beginning in 1883, and she worked closely with Olivia Davidson Washington in administering the girls' curriculum at the school. She was a founding member of the Tuskegee Women's Club and a leader in the woman suffrage movement.

The conferences for farmers at Tuskegee and for intellectuals in Atlanta were related to the formation of many new African-American professional societies and social service organizations in the 1880s and 1890s. They were also related to a long-standing method of grassroots political debate—the holding of conventions. Black ministers, editors, business owners, and intellectuals had been holding state and national conventions to address political events since the 1830s. An important national convention was held in Louisville in 1883, and African Americans in many states—including Arkansas, Georgia, Kansas, Maryland, Rhode Island, Texas, and South Carolina—organized conventions in the 1880s and 1890s for regional black leaders to discuss political policies and conditions. Rejecting Washington's tactic of appeasement and silence on political issues, the state leaders who met at these conventions discussed the role of blacks in party

Teacher and administrator Kelly Miller (far right) was an original member of the American Negro Academy. He is seen here with a Howard University surveying class in 1893. As dean of the College of Arts and Sciences, Miller redesigned the curriculum at Howard and emphasized the social sciences.

politics and demanded that state legislatures and the U.S. Congress respect black people's civil and political rights.

Several rights organizations were outgrowths of the state convention movement. Among them were the National Association of Colored Men, which was organized at a convention in Detroit in January 1896. In a resolution sent to the U.S. Congress, this group announced, "We aim at nothing unattainable, nothing Utopian, not what the society of the future is seeking, but merely what other citizens of this civilization are now enjoying."

T. Thomas Fortune's National Afro-American League, formed in 1890 and revived in new form in 1898 as the Afro-American Council, was another organization that black leaders joined in order to promote equal citizenship rights.

T. Thomas Fortune was a close friend of Booker T. Washington for many years and he supported Washington's platform on industrial education. Washington in turn gave financial support to Fortune's newspaper, the *New York Age.* Politically, however, Fortune was much more openly militant than Washington, and in the North in the 1890s he was one of the most widely recognized advocates for African-American rights. His National Afro-American League had objectives and approaches to problems facing blacks that would be used again by civil rights organizations in the next century. Fortune made the goals of the league clear in the very first sentence of his address to its founding convention: "We are here to-day," he told the audience, "as representatives of 8 million freemen, who know our rights and have the courage to defend them."

The members of the Afro-American League favored public agitation for black rights. At their first convention they demanded an end to lynching and mob violence, the convict lease system, in which black prisoners were hired out to labor in fields, industries, and mines, and the suppression of black people's ability to vote in the South. They also pointed out the unfair distribution of funds to black and white schools and discrimination against black people in public transportation and in public facilities. The league emphasized the importance of black solidarity. It favored separate black economic development, including the formation of black banks, job bureaus, and cooperative business enterprises. Local leagues were founded in several states in 1889, most of them in large cities such as San Francisco and Boston, and in other areas of the Northeast and Midwest. Both men and women were urged to participate. "In the League," Fortune said, "a woman is just as good as a man."

The National Afro-American Council came into being at a convention in Rochester, New York, in September 1898. It was important in large part for its influence and connection to other activist groups that emerged in the years immediately following. Its platform emphasizing civil rights and suffrage, for example, foreshadowed the goals of the Niagara Movement, a black intellectual group that W. E. B. Du Bois would help to found in 1905. That, in turn, led to the National Association for the Advancement of Colored People (NAACP), founded in 1910, which would serve as a major source for equal rights advocacy for decades. And, although Booker T. Washington did not participate in the founding sessions of the council, the group's policies and public statements were soon dominated by Washington and his colleagues. The National Afro-American Council remained active until 1906, but its militancy was tempered by Washington's influence, and much of the energy that had gone into its economic programs was diverted to Washington's National Negro Business League, founded in 1900 in Boston.

The need for such a business league, and the importance of black consumers buying goods and services they needed from black-owned businesses, had been voiced a few years before by W. E. B. Du Bois at one of the Atlanta University conferences. Du Bois later became the director of the Afro-American Council's Negro Business Bureau, where he instituted a plan to establish local business leagues around the country. But it was Washington who held more power in the council organization, and thus he who acted upon the idea for a national group to promote black commerce. The late 1880s and 1890s were a time when many new black businesses were started and when growing black urban populations brought increased business to black grocers, barbers, butchers, hotel and retail shop owners, undertakers, and real estate dealers. Black banks and insurance companies, cemeteries, and building and loan companies were also founded.

One of the issues that most concerned T. Thomas Fortune in the first year of the Afro-American Council's activism was the effect of American imperialism on people of color. He was especially concerned about the impact that the United States' war against Spain and its intervention in the Philippines in 1898 and 1899 had on Cubans, Puerto Ricans, and Filipinos.

Many Cubans had immigrated to the United States since the 1860s, when the Cuban-owned United States–based cigar industry expanded and attracted many workers. Emigration increased during periods of unrest and economic depression in Cuba, including the years of the failed Cuban insurrection (or Ten Years War) from 1868 to 1878 and the Spanish-American War (or War of Independence) of 1895–98. During the Ten Years War many of Havana's middle-class creole entrepreneurs and professionals moved to New York to do business, and in the 1890s Spanish- and Afro-Cuban émigrés provided a multiracial work force for their cigar factories. Afro-Cuban émigrés, who made up about one-fifth of all Cuban immigrants to the United States in the 1880s and 1890s, became part of existing Cuban-immigrant communities of tobacco workers in Florida, Louisiana, and New York. In 1895 more than 5,000 Cubans of color lived in Key West, Florida, and thousands more in company towns such as Ybor City that were established on the outskirts of Tampa, Florida.

When middle-class mulatto Cuban immigrants (mixed-race people of primarily African and Spanish descent), who had occupied a distinct place in the social strata of Cuba, arrived in the United States, they were confronted with Jim Crow practices that forced them to redefine themselves as either white or black. Some Cubans of color chose a white identity because of the social and economic privileges such a choice made possible. Others chose, out of race pride and cultural unity, to associate with African Americans and Caribbean immigrants of African heritage, such as those from Puerto Rico and the Dominican Republic.

The Spanish-American War, which began in 1895, was partly a business matter. Spanish control of territory in the New World had been gradually decreased in the late 19th century to domination of the islands of Cuba and Puerto Rico. As the end of the century approached, Cubans increasingly desired their political independence. But even as Spanish influence was waning, American business interests had invested many millions of dollars in Cuban plantations and refineries.

When Cubans revolted against Spanish rule in 1895, the United States had a strong economic interest in controlling the outcome of events. News of the terrible suffering of Cubans who were forced from their homes and who faced starvation and disease during the conflict also made many Americans favor U.S. intervention. Many African Americans sympathized with the Cuban rebels, and most cautiously supported U.S. involvement in the war. Others worried that overthrowing Spain and replacing her influence in the Caribbean with that of the United States would only result in the extension of Jim Crow racial discrimination beyond American borders. The coming of the war also raised issues about black patriotism, pointing up the irony of black soldiers serving abroad in the service of a country that did not grant them full citizenship rights at home. Nevertheless, many thousands of African Americans volunteered for service.

The Spanish-American War was one more arena in which African Americans demonstrated leadership in the 1890s. When the war against Spain began in April 1898, Charles Young, a West Point graduate, was the only black commissioned officer in the U.S. armed forces. Young was a friend of W. E. B. Du Bois and had taught with him at Wilberforce University. A lieutenant when the war began, he was promoted to the rank of major (in 1916 he became a colonel). Despite severe racial discrimination within the armed services, by war's end there were more than 100 African-American officers commissioned at the rank of first or second lieutenant. The majority of black volunteer units, including outfits from North

At the start of the Spanish-American War in 1898, Charles Young was the only black commissioned officer in the U.S. armed forces. A graduate of West Point, Young advanced to the rank of colonel.

Carolina, Massachusetts, and Illinois, had black officers in positions of command. Because the war only lasted a few months (it ended in July 1898), most of these 8,000 to 10,000 black volunteers never left military bases in the United States.

In the years between the Civil War and the Spanish-American War, four regular units of African-American soldiers, including the 9th and 10th Cavalries and the 24th and 25th Infantries, had been active in the U.S. Army in the West. These were the black regiments that were sent to Cuba in June 1898. The soldiers in these units, called "Buffalo Soldiers" by Native Americans in the West, were dubbed "Smoked Yankees" by the Cubans of African descent who met them during the war. They served with distinction in the key battles, most notably at El Caney, Las Guasimas, and San Juan Hill. In the last, they were instrumental in winning the battle for which Theodore Roosevelt and his Rough Riders gained fame. Black sailors also served aboard U.S. Navy ships, and some 2,000 black men enlisted in the Navy during the war.

The question of leadership within the military became one of the largest issues of the war for African Americans. John Mitchell, Jr., the pub-

Wearing their full-dress uniforms, African-American members of the 25th U.S. Infantry stand at attention outside their barracks at Fort Randall in the Dakota Territory.

lisher of the *Richmond Planet,* a black newspaper in Virginia, coined the phrase "No officers, no fight!" It neatly summed up the African-American demand that blacks be promoted to positions of command and that black units be headed by black officers.

Blacks around the United States were well informed about the war from a black perspective because hundreds of black soldiers wrote home to African-American newspapers about their experiences. M. W. Saddler, a first sergeant in Company D of the 25th Infantry in Cuba, wrote to the Indianapolis, Indiana, paper the *Freeman*, which published his letter on August 27, 1898. He addressed the widespread feeling among the black soldiers that the white press was not doing justice to the black contribution to the war. He also expressed his desire for the military to do right by black leadership. "I wish to call attention to the heroic part the Twenty-fifth United States Infantry played in compelling the surrender of Santiago," he began his letter. "We have no reporter in the division and it appears that we are coming up unrepresented." He then told the story of the battle. For Saddler, the most important thing was what he and his fellow soldiers had proved to the world. The bravery of the black infantry members in the battle for Santiago showed the "world that true patriotism is in the minds of the sons of Ham.... All we need is leaders of our own race to make war records," he concluded, "so that their names may go down in history as a reward for the price of our precious blood."

American Negro Academy member Paul Laurence Dunbar captured the spirit of these men's letters in a poem. In "The Conquerors, The Black Troops in Cuba," Dunbar paid tribute to black heroism. He also wrote about the power of the word, praising the statements about manhood and citizenship that black soldiers had made both on the field by their example and off the field in their letters about their experiences.

> Round the wide earth, from the
>   red field your valour has won,
> Blown with the breath of the
>   far-speaking gun,
>   Goes the word,
> Bravely you spoke through the battle
>   cloud heavy and dun,
> Tossed though the speech toward
>   the mist-hidden sun,
>   The world heard.

Journalism was yet another outlet that leading African Americans used as a medium of self-expression. As we have seen, newspapers provided space for common people, like the soldiers who fought in Cuba, to describe the world as they saw it and share their opinions on political issues. Activism through the spoken and written word was often linked through newsprint. For example, Victoria Earle Matthews invited Ida B. Wells to give her landmark speech about lynching because Matthews had read Wells's newspaper articles about lynching. Matthews, like Wells, worked as a journalist. Under the pen name Victoria Earle, she wrote for such papers as the *Brooklyn Eagle* and the *New York Times*. But more importantly, she wrote articles for some of the major African-American newspapers of the day, including the *Richmond Planet,* the *Washington Bee,* and the *Cleveland Gazette.* When she read Ida B. Wells's articles about lynching, she was working regularly for T. Thomas Fortune's *New York Age.* The influence of black newspapers was not restricted to the Northeast and the South. By 1900 more than 60 such newspapers had been founded in the states west of the Mississippi River, including Emmett J. Scott's *Texas Freeman.*

A group of black soldiers at their base in New York before they were shipped to Cuba to fight in the Spanish-American War.

African Americans also emerged as leading figures in sports and the performing arts, and in the writing of fiction and poetry. Some of these cultural leaders achieved stature while accommodating their art to white audiences. Other leading black writers and performers chose to confront the prejudices of white audiences head-on. Some of them reacted to white racism by choosing to perform primarily for black audiences. Others used their art, performances, and writings to educate their mixed audiences about the range of black experience and to dispel negative stereotypes about black people.

Black jockeys dominated the winner's circle at the prestigious Kentucky Derby in Louisville, Kentucky, in the 1880s and 1890s. Isaac Murphy, nationally recognized as America's finest rider at that time, was the first man in history to win the Kentucky Derby three times—in 1884, 1890, and 1891. At the same time that black athletes were excelling before large crowds in the sport of horse racing, African Americans were emerging as stars in the fields of music and musical theater. Soprano Sissieretta Jones was hailed as the "Black Patti" in tribute to the beauty of her voice, which critics compared to that of the much-acclaimed Italian opera singer Adelina Patti. Jones sang at Madison Square Garden in New York in 1892 and soon after appeared at the White House in a command performance for

Isaac Murphy, third from right, was the first man in history to win the Kentucky Derby three times. Black jockeys dominated this event during the 1880s and 1890s.

President Benjamin Harrison. The next year, she made a grand tour of Europe. She returned to the United States and was barred because of her race from performing at the Metropolitan Opera in New York. (The ban against blacks appearing at the nation's most prestigious opera house remained until 1955, when Marian Anderson became the first African American to perform there.)

Jones adapted to the white prejudice that excluded her from major opera houses by forming an all-black concert company called Black Patti's Troubadours. The group, with which Jones appeared as a soloist, presented arias from such operas as *Lucia de Lammermoor* and *Il Trovatore* as well as dancing and selections of popular music. The group went on tour and performed for 16 years for black audiences in small towns and cities.

New images of blacks were also being presented to white and black audiences in other areas of musical theater and in literature. The lyricism that Sissieretta Jones was famous for portraying with her voice also filled the work of the late 19th century's most prominent African-American poet, Paul Laurence Dunbar. Dunbar was an elevator operator in Dayton, Ohio, when he began publishing his poetry. He had been a

Despite a triumphant tour of Europe's opera houses, where audiences hailed the beauty of her voice, Sissieretta Jones was barred from appearing in many opera houses in the United States because of her race. She formed her own all-black concert company, Black Patti's Troubadours, and performed across the country.

member of the literary society and editor of the school newspaper at Central High School in Dayton, and his first poems were published in newspapers. His first collection of poems, *Oak and Ivy*, was published in 1892, followed by *Majors and Minors* (1895), *Lyrics of Lowly Life* (1896), and *Lyrics of the Hearth-side* (1899). He also wrote short stories and novels. Dunbar's poetry received great critical acclaim. It also became very popular for African-American schoolchildren to memorize his poems and recite them in public programs, so that he was well known among both the intellectual elite and poorer people. He wrote poems in standard English and using black dialect speech, combining lyrical themes of love and death with depictions of African-American life and tributes to outstanding African-American leaders such as Frederick Douglass and Alexander Crummell.

Although most of Dunbar's work was not political in theme, he wrote what would become one of the most important protest poems in all of African-American literature. Called "We Wear the Mask," the poem talks about the dual nature of African-American existence, in which blacks exhibited a certain code of amiable outer behavior to meet white expectations, while underneath that accommodating outer demeanor, true thoughts and feelings lay hidden. Published in *Lyrics of Lowly Life*, "We Wear the Mask" goes like this:

> We wear the mask that grins and lies,
> It hides our cheeks and shades our eyes,—
> This debt we pay to human guile;
> With torn and bleeding hearts we smile,
> And mouth with myriad subtleties
>
> Why should the world be over-wise,
> In counting all our tears and sighs?
> Nay, let them only see us, while
> We wear the mask.

We smile, but, O great Christ, our cries
To thee from tortured souls arise.
We sing, but oh the clay is vile
Beneath our feet, and long the mile;
But let the world dream otherwise,
We wear the mask!

In addition to writing poetry, Paul Laurence Dunbar was involved in musical theater as a songwriter. He and composer Will Marion Cook wrote an operetta called *Clorindy* in 1898. When *Clorindy* went on a tour of East Coast cities that September, it starred two of Dunbar and Cook's friends from New York, Bert Williams and George Walker. Bert Williams was born in the British West Indies and went to high school in Riverside, California. He and Walker began their career as a duo in a minstrel company in San Francisco in 1893. They developed their own comedy act, and by the mid-1890s they were leading men in New York variety productions. Walker's wife, Aida Overton Walker, had been a dancer with the Black Patti Troubadours. She appeared in all the Williams and Walker shows and choreographed their major numbers.

Williams and Walker's fame did not come without a price. Their act played to white stereotypes about blacks. Walker was the dandy, appearing in elaborately designed fancy street clothes that made fun of black consumerism and middle-class aspirations. Williams, who had never lived in the American South, played a Southern tramplike figure who sang in dialect and played the banjo. A light-skinned man, he also appeared on stage in blackface, which meant that he rubbed burnt cork on his face to make it look darker and applied makeup to exaggerate his African features. White actors had long been doing the same thing to caricature black people in minstrel and variety shows, and thus Williams's makeup fulfilled white audiences' expectations of what a black person should look like on stage. For Williams, who in real life was a dignified and quiet man, his on-stage persona was one in which he quite literally wore the mask.

The folk dialect that was used in stage by acts like Williams and Walker's, and in popular music like the songs written by Cook and Dunbar, also was used by African Americans who wrote short stories and novels. This was true for the two most prominent African-American authors of the 1890s, Charles Waddell Chesnutt and Frances Ellen Watkins Harper. Both of these writers used dialect when creating dialogue for black folk charac-

Paul Laurence Dunbar was working as an elevator operator in Dayton, Ohio, when he began publishing his critically acclaimed poetry. By 1898 his work had brought him international fame. Booker T. Washington called him the "Poet Laureate of the Negro People."

The team of George Walker (right) and Bert Williams was one of the most popular African-American acts in vaudeville. Despite their celebrity, they continued to face segregation in the hotels and eating establishments of the cities where they performed. After Walker's death, Williams became the nation's first big-name African-American star as a featured performer with the Ziegfeld Follies.

ters who were illiterate or lacked formal education. For these characters an oral, rather than a written, tradition was paramount. Educated and middle-class characters, by contrast, spoke standard English in these writers' books.

Charles Chesnutt was the principal of a school in Fayetteville, North Carolina, before he moved north to Cleveland, Ohio, and went into business as a lawyer and courtroom stenographer. He wrote several novels and stories, including *The Marrow of Tradition* (1901), a novel about Jim Crow practices and white violence that he began when he heard about the massacre of blacks that occurred in Wilmington, North Carolina, in conjunction with the November 1898 elections.

Chesnutt's book *The Conjure Woman,* published in 1899, was a collection of seven stories about a plantation in North Carolina. The stories were told by an elderly black man named Uncle Julius to the new, post–Civil War owners of the land, white Northerners named John and Annie. They were stories with a double message. On one hand, they educated John and Annie about the realities of black life under slavery. They were tales about the separation of husband and wife, mother and child, or of the cruelty of white overseers. One conveyed the message that a man is not a mule.

At the same time, these fables about the past relayed a message or moral that shaped John and Annie's decision making in the present in ways that benefited the local black community. One tale is about a woman who turned her husband into a tree in order to be able to keep him near her. Hearing the story made John and Annie change their plans to tear down an old building on their property, and soon Julius and his neighbors began to use the old building as a meeting place for their church.

Just as the tales in themselves had meaning on two levels, so Uncle Julius's character had more than one side. Though he pretended to be servile and obedient, Julius in reality was a very wise and shrewd man. In the stories Julius testifies to an alternative way of understanding and seeing the world, including its spiritual or supernatural dimensions, that the white characters are slow to comprehend.

Frances Ellen Watkins Harper, the other great black writer of the 1890s, was, like Paul Laurence Dunbar, primarily a poet. She was also a leading antislavery lecturer and a supporter of temperance and woman suffrage. She captured the connection between literacy and self-sufficiency in her poem "Aunt Chloe: Learning to Read":

> And I longed to read my Bible,
> For precious words it said;
> But when I begun to learn it,
> Folks just shook their heads,
>
> And said there is no use trying,
> Oh! Chloe, you're too late;
> But as I was rising sixty,
> I had no time to wait.
> So I got a pair of glasses,
> And straight to work I went,
> And never stopped till I could read
> The hymns and Testament.

Then I got a little cabin
A place to call my own—
And I felt as independent
As the queen upon her throne.

Just as Sissieretta Jones sought to present a new image of black womanhood in music, so Harper's *Iola Leroy* (1892), one of the first novels published by an African-American woman, was written in part to dispel stereotypes that whites had about black women. *Iola Leroy* protested derogatory ideas that whites held about black women's social worth and morality by placing at its center an able and intelligent black woman protagonist whose actions and thoughts were full of virtue. The novel's heroine, Iola Leroy, is a well-educated, middle-class woman who devotes her life to the uplift of her people. Harper also used the story to address a series of injustices in African-American history and demonstrate ways in which elite African Americans in the decades after the Civil War developed systems of self-help. For example, she named her main character Iola, the pen name used by Ida B. Wells for her newspaper articles. When Wells spoke at Lyric Hall in New York in 1892, the word Iola had been emblazoned in lights behind her on the stage.

Frances Harper's *Iola Leroy* was published in the same year as two other key works written by African-American women: Ida B. Wells's *Southern Horrors*, an exposé about lynching, and Anna Julia Cooper's *A Voice from the South*, a treatise on the status of women in African-American society. Each of these works, and the lives of each of the women who wrote them, proved that African-American leadership was not just male, but female. Indeed, the 1890s produced so many extraordinary African-American women leaders and organizations that it became known as the "Woman's Era."

CHAPTER 6

WOMAN'S ERA: "STRONG IN A LOVE OF JUSTICE"
◇ ◇ ◇

Today we stand on the threshold of woman's era, and woman's work is grandly constructive. . . . Not the opportunity of discovering new worlds, but that of filling this old world with fairer and higher aims than the greed of gold and the lust of power, is hers. . . . She should be as strong in a love of justice and humanity as the warrior is in his might.

—Frances Ellen Watkins Harper, "Woman's Political Future," a speech at the Women's Congress, World's Columbian Exposition, Chicago, 1893

Spelman Seminary's missionary training class of 1895. Founded in 1881 with financial help from the Woman's American Baptist Home Mission Society, Spelman offered education to black women interested in becoming teachers, nurses, missionaries, and church workers.

In 1893, a year after her novel *Iola Leroy* was published, the veteran lecturer Frances Ellen Watkins Harper stood on the podium at the World's Congress of Representative Women in Chicago. The Women's Congress, as it was known, was held in conjunction with the World's Columbian Exposition, or Chicago World's Fair. Just as the Atlanta Exposition was held to celebrate the economic resurgence of the American South, so the Chicago World's Fair was organized to laud the industrial and cultural achievements of the Americas in the eyes of the world. Exhibition halls were set up to show advancements in many types of fields, and one hall was devoted specifically to the achievements of women. But the Lady Managers, or the board of women who had organized the women's events at the fair, largely excluded African-American women from participating.

When Harper and other black, middle-class women accepted invitations to speak at the Women's Congress, they saw themselves as representatives of all African Americans. They also came to confront the racism that had allowed the Lady Managers of the fair to present only white women's skills and creations as worthy of attention in the Women's Building.

Their speeches, like Harper's novel, Ida B. Wells's pamphlets about lynching, and Anna Julia Cooper's book *A Voice from the South,* represent the bold introduction of black women's voices into the debates within the middle-class African-American community as a whole. Their lectures also represented a defense of black womanhood, answering those who viewed black women as lacking in moral character or as secondary in importance to men. When they appeared in Chicago they challenged white women's racism both by word and example. And they gave voice to principles that they felt black people should hold dear. Among them were the right of young women to educational opportunities equal to those of young men; the right of women—black and white—to vote; and the recognition of the role that women had to play in improving society, both privately within the home and publicly as champions of justice for their race.

At the Women's Congress in Chicago in 1893, Frances Ellen Watkins Harper and the other black women who spoke summed up the issues that were in the minds of many of their sisters. Just as Booker T. Washington's Atlanta speech helped shape race relations well into the 20th century, Harper's speech in Chicago set the agenda for middle-class black women's activism for years ahead. She also gave a name to the 1890s that reflected the rise of a generation of well-educated African-American women to positions of public leadership. She called it the "Woman's Era."

And so it was. Never before had there been so many African-American women speaking their minds in public forums, founding newspapers and schools, and shaping the world around them. In the Woman's Era, middle-class women working in their own towns and cities on behalf of working-class women and the poor developed a national momentum for positive change. Most important, black women's benevolent associations and mothers' and women's clubs joined together into regional federations, and ultimately into the National Association of Colored Women, which was founded in 1896. But the same kind of movement toward the more powerful organization of black women was happening in other ways as well—in the suffrage (right to vote) movement, the temperance (anti-alcohol) movement, and the Baptist church.

Frances Ellen Watkins Harper earned an international reputation as a poet, lecturer, and proponent of the antislavery, temperance, suffrage, and women's rights causes. Her 1892 novel, Iola Leroy, *was a powerful appeal for justice and dignity in the post-Reconstruction era.*

Individual women such as Ida B. Wells, Josephine St. Pierre Ruffin, Frances Harper, and Anna Julia Cooper participated in the cause by writing and publishing newspaper articles and books, and by lecturing to many different kinds of audiences. By getting involved in all these areas of organizing, middle-class African-American women supported similar values. They believed that women had a crucial moral contribution to make in improving the world, and that by working together they could bring about reforms that would benefit African Americans in all walks of life.

In her speech in Chicago, Harper argued that the "world has need of all the spiritual aid that woman can give for the social advancement and moral development of the human race." Women's abilities and contributions were far too valuable to waste, and to talk only of the advancement of men and their greater opportunities was not sufficient. "The world cannot move without woman's sharing in the movement," Harper told her audience, "and to help give a right impetus to that movement is woman's highest privilege." Harper, like her colleague Anna Julia Cooper, believed that women represented a force for good that would counteract men's tendencies toward destructiveness, war, and violence. She also argued, along with Cooper, that women should enter public and economic life. "By opening doors of labor," Harper said of black women trying to broaden the types of work they were allowed to do, "woman has become a rival claimant for at least some of the wealth monopolized by her stronger brother." She called for the "ballot in the hands of woman," which would add direct political power to the already existing influence of women in the home, the church pew, the classroom, and the press. She spoke of the male-led worlds of business and the military, the "increase of wealth, the power of armies," being nothing in contrast to the basic social needs of "good homes, of good fathers, and good mothers." She warned of the effects of intemperance, or heavy drinking, upon families, and she castigated lynching. She called on white women as well as black women to "demand justice, simple justice, as the right of every race; to brand with everlasting infamy the lawless and brutal cowardice that lynches, burns, and tortures your own countrymen."

In presenting this political platform, Harper echoed many of the opinions expressed by Anna Julia Cooper in *A Voice from the South*, published the previous year. Cooper, too, questioned the top-to-bottom structure of power that led one nation to attempt to conquer another, or one race to consider itself superior to another. She compared these attitudes of dominance to the ways that intellectual and political opportunities were open to men but closed to women, and to the fact that white women's prejudices against black women tarnished and limited existing movements for women's political rights. She stated that no civilization could rise higher than its women, and that the key to progress for any society was the development of its women's full rights and opportunities. She argued strongly for women's access to higher education and intellectual achievement, and for the economic independence of women that such training would permit.

Cooper, like Harper, was one of the African-American women who spoke to the international audience at the Chicago Women's Congress. She had taught school in her home state of North Carolina before graduating from the "men's" course of study with A.B. (1884) and M.A. (1887) degrees at Oberlin College—one of the first women students to do so. She headed the modern language department at Wilberforce College in Ohio—the same school where American Negro Academy leader W. E. B. Du Bois and military officer Charles Young taught. Later she moved to Washington, D.C., where she became one of the most important educators of her time. She served as principal of the famed M Street High School. She was also one of the first African-American women to obtain a Ph.D. degree, which she earned from the Sorbonne in Paris in 1925, when she was 66.

While Anna Julia Cooper and Frances Watkins Harper, along with educators Fanny Jackson Coppin, Hallie Quinn Brown, and Sarah Early, and women's club activist Fannie Barrier Williams each chose to make their visions of woman-centered social change known by addressing the Women's Congress in person, Ida B. Wells decided not to speak. Instead she protested white racism by putting together a short book, published in Chicago during the World's Fair. She called it *The Reason Why the Colored American Is Not in the World's Columbian Exposition*. Frederick Douglass, who had long supported women's right to vote and other women's causes, wrote the book's introduction.

The book included chapters about slavery, disenfranchisement, and lynching. It also chronicled African-American achievements, including a list of patents granted to black men and women and biographies of black artists, authors, and musicians. It ended with documentation of black people's exclusion from the fair by the white administrators. Wells raised the money to publish the pamphlet by arranging a series of Sunday afternoon meetings among women at different Chicago-area churches. She printed 20,000 copies of the pamphlet, and they were distributed throughout Chicago and by mail.

The same year, Wells traveled to England and Scotland to give lectures about lynching. Frederick Douglass encouraged her to go and loaned her the money to make the trip. "It seemed like an open door in a stone wall," she wrote in her memoirs. Excluded from the South because of her newspaper writings, and having trouble getting people in the North to listen to her, she went across the Atlantic Ocean to speak in cities such as Edinburgh, Liverpool, Manchester, and London. In every speech she gave she educated white British audiences about Jim Crow laws in the American South and the realities of lynching. She succeeded in making the antilynching campaign international. "She has shaken this country like an earthquake," Bishop Henry McNeal Turner wrote of Wells after she completed her tour. She hoped, as she wrote in her autobiography, that the pressure of public opinion from overseas would mean "sentiment will be aroused" at home "and laws enacted which will put a stop to America's disgrace."

Frances Ellen Watkins Harper's speech in Chicago and Ida B. Wells's lectures abroad were both catalysts for more rigorous organization of a national black women's club movement in the mid-1890s. The movement started off with local groups in several different places. Many of these groups began in 1892–93. The Women's Loyal Union had been formed by Victoria Earle Matthews and other middle-class women activists in New York after Wells's Lyric Hall speech in 1892. The Colored Women's League of Washington, D.C., the Women's Era Club of Boston, and the Ida B. Wells Club of Chicago were formed soon after.

Mary Church Terrell, president of the Bethel Literary and Historical Society in Washington, D.C., was one of the founders of the Colored Women's League. The founding statement the league drafted, written in June 1892, summed up the spirit of the middle-class black woman's movement. "Whereas," it read, "in Union there is Strength, and Whereas, we, as a people, have been and are the subject of prejudice, proscription, and injustice, the more successful, because the lack of unity and organization, Resolved, That we, the colored women of Washington, associate ourselves together." The Colored Women's League soon expanded by opening branches in other cities, including Richmond and Norfolk, Virginia, and Newport, Rhode Island.

Journalist Josephine St. Pierre Ruffin headed the Boston Woman's Era Club. Originally called the New Era Club when it was founded in February 1893, it took the name of the Woman's Era that Frances Harper had used in her speech. In March 1894 Ruffin began publishing a monthly journal of opinion called the *Woman's Era*. Black women activists from all over the country—Mary Church Terrell of Washington, Alice Ruth Moore of New Orleans (who later married the poet Paul Laurence Dunbar, and became herself a noted literary figure under the name Alice Dunbar Nelson), Victoria Earle Matthews of New York, and Fannie Barrier Williams of Chicago—contributed to the journal, which served as a forum for the new women's movement.

One of the major concerns voiced in Anna Julia Cooper's *A Voice from the South* and many of the black women's speeches at the World's Fair was whites' habit of questioning black women's sexual morality. Ida B. Wells always made this issue a part of her lectures on lynching. Cooper spoke for the other women activists when she wrote that unwanted sexual advances were typically made by whites, not blacks. Speaking of attitudes about rape, she said that the blame had been misplaced on black people. Historically, whites were primarily responsible for sexual offenses against blacks, not vise versa. "Overtures for forced association in the past history of these two races were not made by the manacled black man, nor by the silent and suffering black woman!" she declared. Black women's outrage over this issue of their alleged immorality was a major impetus to the formation of the national black women's movement.

It happened this way. A white American journalist—a man from Missouri—wrote a letter in which he attacked Ida B. Wells's character because she had spoken out against Southern lynching on her trips abroad, and in which he demeaned the character of black women in general. Copies of the offensive letter were circulated among women activists in the antilynching movement in England and passed on to club leaders in the United States. When Josephine St. Pierre Ruffin received a copy of the letter, she decided to take action. She sent out a circular and on the editorial page of the June 1895 issue of *Woman's Era* printed a call for a big meeting of women. "To all colored women of America, members of any society or not," she wrote, "Let Us Confer Together." The result was the First National Conference of the Colored Women of America.

The conference convened in Boston at the end of July 1895. In her keynote speech, Ruffin outlined the many reasons for getting black women from all over the nation together. "In the first place," she said, "we need to feel the cheer and inspiration of meeting each other, we need to gain the courage and fresh life that comes from the mingling of congenial souls, of those working for the same ends." Ruffin also told her audience that they

The National Federation of Afro-American Women was an alliance formed by 54 previously independent women's groups from 14 different states. It held its first national convention in Boston in 1895. The group soon evolved into the National Association of Colored Women.

needed to take a united stand and make their voices heard: "Too long have we been silent under unjust and unholy charges," she said, referring to slanderous accusations against middle-class black women. The women delegates decided to form a new organization. They named it the National Federation of Afro-American Women and elected Margaret Murray Washington, the Tuskegee activist, as president.

Meanwhile, other groups were forming. The following summer, in July 1896, the National Federation of Afro-American Women and the Washington, D.C.–based National League of Colored Women merged with more than 100 other women's clubs to form a new coalition. It was called the National Association of Colored Women. Frances Harper was at this historic meeting, a representative of older, former antislavery activists, as was the great elderly abolitionist Harriet Tubman, who had helped many

African Americans escape slavery during the Civil War. Frederick Douglass's only daughter, Rosetta Sprague, participated. Ida B. Wells, who had recently married and changed her name to Ida B. Wells-Barnett, came with her new baby son to chair one of the conference committees. Mary Church Terrell was elected president of the new national organization. When the NACW met for its second annual conference in 1897, it moved its meeting south to Nashville, Tennessee, and began publication of a periodical, *National Notes*.

Mary Church Terrell had graduated from Oberlin College with Anna Julia Cooper and, like Cooper, lived in Washington, D.C. She grew up in Memphis, Tennessee, and like Ida B. Wells, had been a close friend of Peoples' Grocery owner Thomas Moss. Her husband, Robert Terrell, was a close associate of Booker T. Washington and the Terrell family was well-to-do. Mary Church Terrell's election as president was questioned by some. To some of the more progressive delegates she represented an overly conservative approach to social issues and, as a very rich woman, she had a sensibility that was very remote from the lives of the masses of black Americans. Nevertheless, she headed the National Association of Colored Women from its inception in 1896 until 1901.

The motto of the NACW, "Lifting As We Climb," reflected the perspective of the middle-class women who made up the movement. They saw themselves improving the conditions and behavior of lower-class women as they instituted social reforms and defended the respectability of women like themselves. The activities of the NACW were similar to the kinds of outreach that was already being done in local areas through churches, settlement houses, and women's neighborhood groups. Under Terrell's leadership the NACW members emphasized early childhood education, especially the establishment of kindergartens and day nurseries.

In doing so, they were following a philosophy of social change that Anna Julia Cooper had described metaphorically in *A Voice from the South.* Cooper wrote about beginning at the root in order to make healthy and vigorous plants grow, and so the club women believed that change for future generations of African Americans had to begin with the children. They also actively supported the major women's progressive movements, including suffrage, temperance, self-help, and moral reform.

The National Association of Colored Women was formed in 1896 by the merger of the National League of Colored Women and the National Federation of Afro-American Women. Representing more than 100 women's clubs, the new coalition proved to be a powerful promoter of self-help, equity, and justice for black women.

← COMING! ←

ON _____

Mrs. Mary Church Terrell

First President of the National Association of Colored Women,
Member of the Board of Education of the District
of Columbia for Eleven Years,

IN A LECTURE, ENTITLED:

As president of the NACW, Mary Church Terrell was a widely sought-after speaker. Her conservative views on social and racial issues placed her at odds with other more militant members of the group such as Ida B. Wells.

In a time when most black Americans lived in the South and made their living in agriculture, the leadership, and much of the membership, of the NACW was largely based in the North and among urban women. The middle-class clubwomen had economic opportunities and life-style choices that were not available to a majority of black women. There were also internal splits among the ranks of NACW leaders. Ideological rivalries existed between women such as Mary Church Terrell, who was often compared to Booker T. Washington in politics and temperament, and more fiery and militant members such as Ida B. Wells-Barnett. Geographic rivalries also existed between the various NACW leaders from different Northern cities, whether Boston, Chicago, Washington, D.C., or New York, each of whom had a claim to the leadership of the original club movement. But despite these internal differences, the NACW functioned as a clearinghouse for black women's community action until the 1930s.

Black women's involvement in the temperance movement straddled the line between the secular politics of the women's club movement and the religious convictions that led black women of all classes to work in their communities through their churches. Temperance, or the movement to moderate or ban the use of alcohol, was part of the self-help aspect of black institution building. The misuse of alcohol, temperance leaders argued, drained families of needed income, took attention away from children, and led to domestic violence. Women and children often paid the emotional and physical price of men's drinking, and men who socialized at bars and pool halls were not turning their attention to more constructive things. They also helped feed white stereotypes about nonproductive black men.

When the African Methodist Episcopal church sponsored a symposium about temperance in 1891, it was Frances Harper who gave the keynote address. In her talk, published in the *AME Church Review*, she told supporters to "consecrate, educate, agitate, and legislate." Harper had long worked with the Women's Christian Temperance Union (WCTU). She was a city, state, and eventually, national WCTU organizer for temperance in black communities. In her poetry in the 1880s, she wrote about the destructive effects on families caused by the abuse of alcohol, and in 1888 she wrote an essay called "The Women's Christian Temperance Union and the Colored Woman." She told of moral influence women could have in the home and of the direct-action tactic in which "saloons were visited, hardships encountered, insults, violence and even imprisonment endured by women, brave to suffer and strong to endure."

Harper's relatively positive experience in regional chapters of the WCTU contrasted with that of Josephine St. Pierre Ruffin and Ida B. Wells, both of whom found the white leadership of the WCTU intolerably racist. Wells in particular was appalled at WCTU president Frances Willard's acceptance of the white Southern practice of lynching and negative stereotypes of both black women and men. Despite such prejudices, black women joined black auxiliaries to the white women's union. By 1898, five independent black women's state temperance unions had been founded in the South—in Arkansas, Georgia, North Carolina, Tennessee, and Texas.

The racism and the opposition of white Southern women to integration that characterized the temperance movement also limited the ability of black women to participate in the organized woman suffrage movement. Black women leaders found their own ways of furthering the cause of women's right to vote. Mary Ann Shadd Cary, a Washington, D.C., lawyer and a graduate of Howard University, founded the Colored Women's Progressive Franchise Association as an auxiliary of the predominantly white National American Woman Suffrage Association on February 9, 1880. Cary's self-help group supported equal rights for women and made lobbying for suffrage its first priority. Adella Hunt Logan, who led women's sessions at the annual Tuskegee conferences and participated in the Atlanta University conferences, was a very light-skinned black person. She used this to her advantage in "passing" as white in order to attend National American Woman Suffrage Association conventions in the segregated South. She then related what had happened in the meetings to fellow black

Her role as an organizer for the Chicago Working Women's Union offered Lucy Parsons a large audience for her powerful, revolutionary speeches. An anarchist and socialist, Parsons struggled to draw people's attention to the problems of the working class.

activists in Southern states. Mary Church Terrell was a life member of NAWSA in the North and appeared as a speaker at many of the organization's national meetings, including those in 1898 and 1900. Terrell was among those who used her upper-class, college-educated status as an argument for the right of others like her to vote, arguing that the franchise should not be withheld from black women of culture and learning.

While Mary Church Terrell and other conservative clubwomen were advocating the rights of privileged black women, Lucy Parsons championed the cause of working people and the poor. Parsons moved in entirely different circles from the black reformers who united into women's organizations in the 1890s. Parsons was born in Waco, Texas, of mixed African, Indian, and Mexican ancestry. She married a white man named Albert Parsons, and together they entered a life of political activism. Just as the antilynching and women's movements foreshadowed many of the issues and approaches of the civil rights and women's liberation movements of the 20th century, Lucy Parsons's kind of activism set an example for black people's involvement in the various movements of the American Left.

Lucy Parsons was an anarchist and socialist. She and her husband lived in primarily white-ethnic, working-class neighborhoods in Chicago, where she worked as a seamstress. Albert Parsons was a leader in the International Working People's Association, and both he and Lucy were members of the Knights of Labor. Lucy Parsons wrote revolutionary essays about homelessness, violence, unemployment, and working people's rights for her husband's newspaper, *Alarm,* and she became an organizer for the Chicago Working Women's Union.

She was known for her electrifying speeches, and as part of her work with the Knights of Labor she organized mostly white Chicago women in the sewing trades in support of an eight-hour workday. When several hundred of the sewing women marched through the streets of Chicago in May 1886, the *Chicago Tribune* called them the "Shouting Amazons," a reference to the legendary woman warriors. In 1891, Lucy Parsons joined the ranks of black women editors when she began publishing her own newspaper, *Freedom.* Unlike the periodicals of the black woman's movement, *Freedom* put class, rather than race or gender, at the forefront of the fight for justice.

Nannie Helen Burroughs bridged the worlds between the working women whom Parsons championed and the middle-class realm of the black women's club movement. Much of her activism took place within the black church. Most of the African-American women who became involved as activists in the woman's era had experience as community workers through their churches, and much of the spirit of reform that filled the 1890s emerged originally from self-help messages within the church. It is fitting, then, that women's organization building and feminist thought in the last decade of the 19th century also

had an impact on the way women were viewed within the black church. The growing awareness about women's abilities that had sprung from the church and blossomed in middle-class, secular organizations was plowed back in to enrich the soil of religious institutions. Nannie Helen Burroughs was only 21 years old when she gave a speech called "How the Sisters Are Hindered from Helping" at the annual National Baptist Convention in Richmond, Virginia, in September 1900. Her plea for a more powerful and united presence for black women within the Baptist church led to the

Nannie Helen Burroughs organized thousands of women within the black church to work for women's rights, desegregation, and educational opportunities.

founding of the Woman's Convention, an auxiliary to the National Baptist Convention. The Woman's Convention, with more than 1 million members, proved to be the largest black women's organization in America. Through it, church women set their own policies and provided their own national leaders.

In the late 19th century, in the midst of Jim Crow repression and the loss of many political and civil rights, black people turned to their own institutions and sought justice in their own ways. In 1893, Frances Ellen Watkins Harper spoke of being on the threshold of a woman's era. In 1900, black men and women stood together on the cusp of a new century. They had as their foundation the many churches, schools, and organizations they had built, and a legacy of leadership that would carry them into the next decades. Demanding justice, they had found the power to act on their own.

THOUGH JUSTICE SLEEPS
◇ ◇ ◇

In the years between 1880 and 1900, the wonderful promise of a future of freedom that was made to black people by emancipation was broken. That promise was begun by the 1863 Presidential proclamation that ended slavery in the midst of the Civil War. It was forged in society by the reforms of postwar Reconstruction that were attempted in the years between the ratification of the 14th Amendment, which granted citizenship rights to freed people in 1868, and the passage of the Civil Rights Act of 1875. It had been a promise of a new social order, in which African Americans would be full citizens with civil rights and equal opportunities. It was a promise that African Americans could conduct their daily lives with the assurance that those rights would be protected—the assurance of wide-awake and diligent social justice.

Instead, justice slept. It was racism that remained wide awake. In the last two decades of the 19th century, African Americans faced a time of terror, denial, and exclusion. The great majority were consigned to dire poverty—either the poverty suffered by sharecropper families working the land in the countryside, beholden to those who owned the land, or the poverty of migrants to the cities, who searched the streets for manual labor or were denied jobs in occupations for which they had skills.

The devastation that the unchecked racism of the 1880s and 1890s wrought would have long-lasting effects. Many of the patterns of life in the city and in rural towns that were established under conditions of great inequity would remain in force into the 20th century, making the promise of freedom seem ever more elusive. As Memphis grocery store owner Thomas Moss said in 1892 in his final message to black people before his death at the hands of white vigilantes, "Tell my people . . . there is no justice for them here."

Though many freedoms remained out of reach because of the failure of the U.S. government to administer justice, African Americans successfully created and maintained an environment within their own communities that helped them grow and survive. They made their own brand of liberty through their activism and their faith. When John Solomon Lewis's family claimed their own land in Kansas, or Bishop Henry McNeal Turner encouraged African Americans to take pride in Africa, the flame of freedom was maintained. When Richard L. Davis organized mineworkers, or black women in New Orleans marched in the streets in support of striking dockworkers, they kindled the light of freedom that illuminated their path. When Booker T. Washington arrived in Tuskegee, Alabama, and started a school in Johanna Bowen Redgrey's church, that light was further kindled. When Ida B. Wells filed a court action against those who threw her off a train on the way to work, or exposed lies about the motivations of lynching, she did it holding the cause of freedom like a torch in her hand. And when black washerwomen in Atlanta organized a boycott, or middle-class African Americans met in literary clubs or formed women's organizations, freedom was there shining beside them. It was always there, despite the broken promise of emancipation, and it was African Americans who maintained it. They remained, as Frances Harper said in the 1890s, "strong in a love of justice."

The actions they took with that strength in the 1880s and 1890s laid the foundation for what was to come. It would be more than half a century—not until the 1950s and 1960s—that the promise of the Civil Rights Act of 1875 would be renewed on a national political level in the modern civil rights movement. And then, too, it would be African Americans—through their churches, their communities, and through the leadership of the schools and organizations that had their roots in the kinds of institutions founded many, many years before—that would make that new wave of hope come to pass.

The message that the African-American activists of the 1880s and 1890s left for those in the 20th century was a clear one. Frances Harper said it at the Chicago Women's Congress in 1893: "Demand justice, simple justice, as the right of every race."

CHRONOLOGY

1879–1881

First major migration of African Americans from the South to Kansas and Western territories ensues.

1880

U.S. Census reports that the African-American population of the United States totals 6,580,793.

JULY 4, 1881

Booker T. Washington opens Tuskegee Institute in Tuskegee, Alabama.

OCTOBER 15, 1883

In *Civil Rights Cases*, the U.S. Supreme Court reverses the 1875 Civil Rights Act.

1884

T. Thomas Fortune founds the *New York Age* newspaper.

MAY 1884

Schoolteacher Ida B. Wells is removed from the Chesapeake, Ohio, and Southwestern Railroad and begins her lawsuit against the racial segregation of railway transportation.

1886

The Knights of Labor reaches its peak membership at 700,000, including between 60,000 and 90,000 African Americans.

MARCH 1888

The Colored Farmers' National Alliance and Cooperative Union is founded in Lovejoy, Texas.

1889

The federal government opens Oklahoma Territory to settlement, and some 7,000 African Americans participate in the land rush.

1890

U.S. Census reports that the African-American population of the United States is 7,488,676.

The National Afro-American League and the all-black town of Langston, Oklahoma Territory, are founded.

1892

Anna Julia Cooper publishes a set of theoretical essays, *A Voice from the South,* and Frances Ellen Watkins Harper publishes her novel *Iola Leroy.*

FEBRUARY 1892

The Populist, or People's, Party emerges as an independent political party with the support of black and white farmers and laborers.

OCTOBER 5, 1892

Ida B. Wells gives landmark speech about lynching at New York City's Lyric Hall; in the same month, she publishes *Southern Horrors: Lynch Law in All Its Phases*.

1893

Cooper, Harper, Fanny Jackson Coppin, Fannie Barrier Williams, and other black women leaders address the Women's Congress at the World's Columbian Exposition in Chicago. Ida B. Wells makes antilynching lecture tour of Great Britain.

FEBRUARY 20, 1895

Abolitionist and women's rights leader Frederick Douglass dies in Washington, D.C.

JUNE 1895

W. E. B. Du Bois receives his Ph.D. from Harvard University, the first African American to do so.

SEPTEMBER 18, 1895

Booker T. Washington delivers "Atlanta Compromise" speech at the Cotton States and International Exposition in Atlanta, Georgia.

MAY 18, 1896

In *Plessy* v. *Ferguson*, U.S. Supreme Court upholds the principle of "separate but equal," providing the federal precedent for state and local racial segregation laws.

JULY 21, 1896

The National Association of Colored Women is organized in Washington, D.C.

JULY 1898

Black troops participate in the Spanish-American War.

1900

U.S. Census reports that the African-American population in the United States is 8,833,994.

AUGUST 23–24, 1900

The National Negro Business League is formed in Boston.

SEPTEMBER 1900

Nannie Helen Burroughs leads the founding of the Women's Convention of the National Baptist Convention in Richmond, Virginia.

FURTHER READING

GENERAL AFRICAN-AMERICAN HISTORY

Aptheker, Herbert, ed. *A Documentary History of the Negro People in the United States.* Vol. 2. *From the Reconstruction to the Founding of the NAACP.* New York: Citadel Press, 1951.

Bennett, Lerone, Jr. *Before the Mayflower: A History of Black America.* 6th rev. ed. New York: Viking Penguin, 1988.

———. *The Shaping of Black America.* New York: Viking Penguin, 1993.

Cooper, Anna Julia. *A Voice from the South.* 1892. Reprint, New York: Oxford University Press, 1988.

Foner, Philip S. *History of Black Americans: From Africa to the Emergence of the Cotton Kingdom.* Westport, Conn.: Greenwood, 1975.

Franklin, John Hope, and August Meier, eds. *Black Leaders of the Twentieth Century.* Urbana: University of Illinois Press, 1982.

Franklin, John H., and Alfred A. Moss, Jr. *From Slavery to Freedom: A History of Negro Americans.* 6th ed. New York: Knopf, 1987.

Gates, Henry L., Jr. *A Chronology of African-American History from 1445–1980.* New York: Amistad, 1980.

Giddings, Paula. *When and Where I Enter: The Impact of Black Women on Race and Sex in America.* New York: Bantam, 1985.

Harding, Vincent. *There Is a River: The Black Struggle for Freedom in America.* San Diego: Harcourt Brace, 1981.

Hine, Darlene C., et al., eds. *Black Women in America.* Brooklyn, N.Y.: Carlson, 1993.

Litwack, Leon, and Meier, August. *Black Leaders of the 19th Century.* Urbana: University of Illinois Press, 1988.

Meltzer, Milton. *The Black Americans: A History in Their Own Words.* Rev. ed. New York: HarperCollins, 1984.

Mintz, Sidney W., and Richard Price. *The Birth of African-American Culture: An Anthropological Perspective.* Boston: Beacon Press, 1992.

Quarles, Benjamin. *The Negro in the Making of America.* 3rd ed. New York: Macmillan, 1987.

AFRICAN AMERICANS IN THE 19TH AND EARLY 20TH CENTURIES

Du Bois, W. E. B. *The Philadelphia Negro.* 1899. Reprint, New York: Schocken, 1967.

Foner, Philip S., ed., *The Life and Writings of Frederick Douglass.* Vol. 4. *Reconstruction and After.* New York: International Publishers, 1955.

Fortune, T. Thomas. *Black and White: Land, Labor, and Politics in the South.* 1884. Reprint, New York: Arno Press, 1968.

Gatewood, Willard B., Jr. *"Smoked Yankees" and the Struggle for Empire: Letters from Negro Soldiers, 1898–1902.* Urbana: University of Illinois Press, 1971.

Guy-Sheftall, Beverly. *Daughters of Sorrow: Attitudes toward Black Women, 1880–1920.* Brooklyn, N.Y.: Carlson, 1990.

Harlan, Louis R., Stuart B. Kaufman, Barbara S. Kraft, Pete Daniel, William M. Welty, and Raymond W. Smock, eds. *The Booker T. Washington Papers.* Vol. 2: 1860–89; Vol. 3: 1889–95; Vol. 4: 1895–98. Urbana: University of Illinois Press, 1972, 1974, 1975.

Harris, Trudier, ed. *Selected Works of Ida B. Wells-Barnett.* New York: Oxford University Press, 1991.

Harris, William H. *The Harder We Run: Black Workers since the Civil War.* New York: Oxford University Press, 1982.

Higginbotham, Evelyn Brooks. *Righteous Discontent: The Women's Movement in the Black Baptist Church, 1880–1920.* Cambridge: Harvard University Press, 1993.

Jacobson, Julius, ed. *The Negro and the American Labor Movement.* Garden City, N.Y.: Anchor/Doubleday, 1968.

Katz, William Loren. *The Black West.* Garden City, N.Y.: Doubleday, 1971.

Lane, Roger. *William Dorsey's Philadelphia and Ours.* New York: Oxford University Press, 1991.

Lerner, Gerda, ed. *Black Women in White America: A Documentary History.* New York: Vintage, 1973.

Lewis, Ronald L. *Black Coal Miners in America: Race, Class, and Community Conflict 1780–1980.* Lexington: University Press of Kentucky, 1987.

Lofgren, Charles A. *The Plessy Case: A Legal-Historical Interpretation.* New York: Oxford University Press, 1987.

Meier, August. *Negro Thought in America, 1880–1915: Racial Ideologies in the Age of Booker T. Washington.* Ann Arbor: University of Michigan Press, 1963.

Moss, Alfred A., Jr. *The American Negro Academy: Voice of the Talented Tenth.* Baton Rouge: Louisiana State University Press, 1981.

Painter, Nell Irvin. *Exodusters: Black Migration to Kansas after Reconstruction.* New York: Knopf, 1976.

Rachleff, Peter. *Black Labor in Richmond, 1865–1890.* Urbana: University of Illinois Press, 1989.

Redkey, Edwin S. *Black Exodus: Black Nationalist and Back-to-Africa Movements, 1890–1910.* New Haven, Conn.: Yale University Press, 1969.

Salem, Dorothy. *To Better Our World: Black Women in Organized Reform, 1890–1920.* Brooklyn, N.Y.: Carlson, 1990.

Shapiro, Herbert. *White Violence and Black Response: From Reconstruction to Montgomery.* Amherst: University of Massachusetts Press, 1988.

BIOGRAPHIES AND AUTOBIOGRAPHIES

Ashbaugh, Carolyn. *Lucy Parsons: American Revolutionary.* Chicago: Charles H. Kerr, 1976.

Boyd, Melba Joyce. *Discarded Legacy: Politics and Poetics in the Life of Frances E. W. Harper, 1825–1911.* Detroit: Wayne State University Press, 1994.

Charters, Ann. *Nobody: The Story of Bert Williams.* New York: Macmillan, 1970.

Duster, Alfreda, ed. *Crusade for Justice: The Autobiography of Ida B. Wells.* Chicago: University of Chicago Press, 1970.

Gentry, Tony. *Paul Laurence Dunbar.* New York: Chelsea House, 1989.

Jones, Beverly Washington. *Quest for Equality: The Life and Writings of Mary Eliza Church Terrell, 1863–1954.* Brooklyn, N.Y.: Carlson, 1990.

Lewis, David Levering. *W. E. B. Du Bois: Biography of a Race, 1868–1919.* New York: Holt, 1993.

Miller, Douglas T. *Frederick Douglass and the Fight for Freedom.* New York: Facts on File, 1988.

Schroeder, Alan. *Booker T. Washington.* New York: Chelsea House, 1992.

Sterling, Dorothy. *Black Foremothers: Three Lives.* Old Westbury, N.Y.: Feminist Press, 1979. Includes profiles of Ida B. Wells-Barnett and Mary Church Terrell.

Thompson, Mildred. *Ida B. Wells-Barnett: An Exploratory Study of an American Black Woman, 1893–1930.* Brooklyn, N.Y.: Carlson, 1990.

Thornbrough, Emma Lou. *T. Thomas Fortune: Militant Journalist.* Chicago: University of Chicago Press, 1972.

Washington, Booker T. *Up from Slavery: An Autobiography.* 1900. Reprint, New York: Oxford University Press, 1995.

AFRICAN-AMERICAN LITERATURE

Andrews, William L., ed. *The Oxford Frederick Douglass Reader.* New York: Oxford University Press, 1996.

Chesnutt, Charles W. *The Conjure Woman.* 1899. Reprint, Ann Arbor: University of Michigan Press, 1969.

Dunbar, Paul Laurence. *The Complete Poems of Paul Laurence Dunbar.* 1913. Reprint, New York: Dodd, Mead, 1970.

Harper, Frances Ellen Watkins. *Iola Leroy.* 1892. Reprint, Boston: Beacon Press, 1987.

———. *Complete Poems of Frances E. W. Harper.* Compiled by Maryemma Graham. New York: Oxford University Press, 1988.

Sundquist, Eric, ed. *The Oxford W. E. B. Du Bois Reader.* New York: Oxford University Press, 1996.

INDEX

Acknowledgments

Special thanks to Nataki Goodall and Evelyn Brooks Higginbotham, who developed the title for this book, and to Elsa Barkley Brown for her kindness. Particular thanks are also due to Nell Irvin Painter, for her accounts of the experiences of Exoduster families and the verse of Sojourner Truth; to Tera Hunter, for references drawn from her study of Atlanta washerwomen; to Eric Arnesen and Peter Rachleff for their work on labor organizing in New Orleans and Richmond; to William Loren Katz for his research on the Black West; and to the Oklahoma Historical Society, for reference to the 1939 Works Progress Administration interview with Agnes Rogers Walker by Alene D. McDowell.

Picture Credits

BARBARA BAIR ◇◇◇

Barbara Bair is a documentary editor with the Jane Addams Papers project in the department of history, Duke University. She previously taught American civilization and literature courses at Brown University and was for several years affiliated with the African Studies Center at the University of California, Los Angeles. She is the associate editor of volumes six and seven of *The Marcus Garvey and Universal Negro Improvement Association Papers,* co-editor of *Wings of Gauze: Women of Color and the Experience of Health and Illness* and *The Papers of Will Rogers, The Early Years: Cherokee Nation, Argentina, and South Africa, 1879–1904,* and a contributing editor to *Africa for the Africans: The Marcus Garvey Papers African Series.*

ROBIN D. G. KELLEY ◇◇◇

Robin D. G. Kelley is professor of history and Africana studies at New York University. He previously taught history and African-American studies at the University of Michigan. He is the author of *Hammer and Hoe: Alabama Communists during the Great Depression,* which received the Eliot Rudwick Prize of the Organization of American Historians and was named Outstanding Book on Human Rights by the Gustavus Myers Center for the Study of Human Rights in the United States. Professor Kelley is also the author of *Race Rebels: Culture, Politics, and the Black Working Class* and co-editor of *Imagining Home: Class, Culture, and Nationalism in the African Diaspora.*

EARL LEWIS ◇◇◇

Earl Lewis is professor of history and Afroamerican studies at the University of Michigan. He served as director of the university's Center for Afroamerican and African Studies from 1990 to 1993. Professor Lewis is the author of *In Their Own Interests: Race, Class and Power in Twentieth Century Norfolk* and co-author of *Blacks in the Industrial Age: A Documentary History.*